Culture Wars

Gerry Lewis

PublishAmerica
Baltimore

First printing

At the specific preference of the author, PublishAmerica allowed this work to remain exactly as the author intended, verbatim, without editorial input.

ISBN: 1-4241-6392-7
PUBLISHED BY PUBLISHAMERICA, LLLP
www.publishamerica.com
Baltimore

Printed in the United States of America

ACKNOWLEDGEMENTS

This book originated as a sermon series I preached in my church in the fall of 2003. I really never thought about putting it in book form at the time. When people began responding positively to my first book—a collection of brief devotionals— I began thinking about writing books.

Knowing that most people are not interested in reading something that sounds like a "sermon", I tried to adjust the text of the chapters to make them more reader friendly. I also wanted not to sound to "preachy" in my delivery. I owe a huge thanks to my daughter, Tova—a much better writer than I—for reading the chapters and giving me feedback through teenager/ young adult eyes.

To Tova and Zeke: You know whether or not your dad is the same person he writes about. Thanks for keeping me honest. I love you.

To Eva Dee: Our Jedi training is ongoing as our young Jedi have started leaving the docking station. You have been and always will be my Jedi princess and hero. I'm yours forever.

To my wonderful church family at EMBC: Thanks for listening to me for the past fifteen years, for trusting me even when you don't understand me, and for encouraging me to grow in my ministry even beyond the scope of our church.

To my fellow Jedi in the AMA: We are seeing some amazing things in our community. Let us not grow weary in doing good. The best is yet to be.

INTRODUCTION

May the Force Be with You

I admit it. I'm a fan of the **Star Wars** movies. Not a "stand in line for hours to see the very first show that opens at midnight, dressed as a Storm Trooper, and knowing the names of all the different Sith lords" fan, I just enjoy the movies. The special effects are amazing and it's kind of silly fun.

But the real reason I like the movies is the Jedi. The Jedi are an interesting group of people. They are an ascetic group, not concerned with politics, power, prestige, or possessions. They live a life of contemplation and service. Their loyalties are not primarily political, but spiritual. They respect, support, and learn from each other. They know that their success relies on the power of The Force.

And they have these really cool light sabers! Ok, that's my favorite part. What an amazing weapon! Defensively, they deflect the shots from the Storm Troopers' blasters or the assault of another saber wielded by a devotee of the Dark Side (the big "sithies"). It is a weapon that must be close at hand to be used, but is most effective against a personal attack.

And then there is The Force. It is the true source of power. The Jedi are effective only as they learn to use it. The Sith gain strength as they learn to harness it for the purposes of the Dark

Side. Light sabers are useless to one who does not use the power of the Force.

And *a long time ago in a galaxy far, far away* the battle for the galaxy rages (and makes a gazillion dollars for George Lucas).

CULTURE WARS

The year is 2205 A.D. A twenty-third century movie maker decides to tell the tale of twenty-first century America. In homage to the most successful movie series of the late twentieth and early twenty-first century, a paragraph of text slowly scrolls from the bottom to the top of the screen against a black, star-lit sky. *A long time ago…*

How would that paragraph introduce twenty-first century America? What values would be displayed among people? What forces drive the culture? What is the spiritual climate? What unifies people? What divides them?

I'm not sure how future historians will chronicle the world we are living in today. We are writing that history every day as we seek to navigate the sometimes unfriendly skies of American culture. I do, however, know plenty of people who are convinced that there was a time when the skies were friendlier—people who long for the "good old days" when Judeo-Christian values were the cultural norms. These were times when you would never hear words like *anti-Christian bias, homo-phobic, intolerant, right-wing fundamentalist,* or *liberal media.*

At least that's what I'm told. As a child of the sixties and a teenager of the seventies, my own recollections are of a culture in transition. Viet Nam and Watergate began the erosion of our trust in political leadership. The ensuing three decades of scandalous behavior among elected officials has done nothing to stop the landslide toward total skepticism. We don't trust anyone anymore.

And what about the church? There was a time when pastors ranked consistently among the most respected people in the community. If you heard it in church, it must be true. If the Christian community is for it, it must be a good thing. And then came outlandish televangelists with more glitz than gospel, Jonestown, the PTL scandal—and now we trust Christians just about as much as we trust politicians. It seems that the church has lost its voice.

Permit me to ask three vital questions:

First, how much difference is there between churchgoers and non-churchgoers in our culture?

Second, which one is influencing the other more—church or culture? In other words, when cultural observers take note of the behavior of those who identify themselves as Christians, is there any noticeable distinction about them—other than what they do for an hour or two on Sunday mornings? It may be that the historical role of evangelical Christians—that of calling the church to faith, involvement and commitment—has been replaced with a current generation of evangelicals who have been less discerning regarding what they bring *from* the culture *into* the church.

Third, what are we, as the church to do? If we are indeed *being influenced* by the culture more than we are *influencing* the culture, what's the answer?

Some might suggest *isolation*. This is what Leonard Sweet refers to as the *hunker in the bunker* mentality.[1] Let's gather up all the people who want to live by traditional Christian values and move away into a commune isolated from the outside world. Then *we'll* be safe and we can just pretend that *they* don't exist. And in so doing, we abandon the culture by removing the remaining Christian influence that exists. No, isolation is not the answer.

Others might suggest *separation*. Let them do their thing and we'll do ours. We'll try to stay as far apart as possible. If our paths have to intersect, we'll nod as politely as possible and continue to remind ourselves (and them) that we are not them. Certainly, there are aspects of our culture from which we must separate ourselves, but separation is only a partial answer.

The only real answer is *transformation*. Look at the following words of Jesus and especially notice the phrases that I have emphasized.

*I am no longer in the world; and yet **they themselves are in the world**, and I come to You. Holy Father, keep them in Your name, the name which You have given Me, that they may be one even as We are. While I was with them, I was keeping them in Your name which You have given Me; and I guarded them and not one of them perished but the son of perdition, so that the Scripture would be fulfilled. But now I come to You; and these things I speak in the world so that they may have My joy made full in themselves. I have given them Your word; and the world has hated them, because they are not of the world, even as I am not of the world. **I do not ask You to take them out of the world**, but to keep them from the evil one. They are not of the world, even as I am not of the world. Sanctify them in the truth; Your word is truth. **As You sent Me into the world, I also have sent them into the world.** For their sakes I sanctify Myself, that they* *themselves also may be sanctified in truth. I do not ask on behalf of these alone, but for those also who believe in Me through their word; that they may all be one; even as You, Father, are in Me and I in You, that they also may be in Us,* **so that the world may believe that You sent Me.**[2]

Wow! Do you see the purpose that Christians have in the culture? We are to behave in such a way—*in* the culture—that those who see us will believe the Jesus we claim to know! And in revealing Him, we'll have a hand in transforming the culture back to what God intends.

But, to what do we return? The Bible says, "*Do not move an ancient boundary stone set up by your forefathers.*"[3]

Someone might read that and say, *See, I told you we needed to go back to the good old days.* But what boundary stones are the right ones to guide twenty-first century life? How about the early American boundary stones—the values of our great-grandparents? Nope, not far enough.

Well, then let's study the early church and the foundations of Christianity and see how they responded to their culture. Still too recent.

Then, obviously, I'm referring to the Ten Commandments. If we would just adopt God's laws as the law of the land, everything would be fine. Not quite there yet.

What, then can possibly bring about the kind of transformation that I'm talking about? Only going all the way back to the heart of God. You see, transformation does not begin with methods, but with relationship.

Then God said, "Let Us make man in Our image, according to Our likeness; and let them rule over the fish of the sea and over the birds of the sky and over the cattle and over all the earth, and over every creeping thing that creeps on the earth." God created man in His own image, in the image of God He created him; male and female He created them.[4]

Then the LORD God formed man of dust from the ground, and breathed into his nostrils the breath of life; and man became a living being. The LORD God planted a garden toward the east, in Eden; and there He placed the man whom He had formed. Out of the ground the LORD God caused to grow every tree that is pleasing to the sight and good for food; the tree of life also in the midst of the garden, and the tree of the knowledge of good and evil.[5]

Then the LORD God said, "It is not good for the man to be alone; I will make him a helper suitable for him."[6]

God created human beings for relationship—relationship with Him and relationship with other humans. Another way of saying that is that God created us for culture. He created us to function within a society that derives its norms—not simply through legislation and powerful enforcement—by means of relationship.

One of the reasons that legislated morality fails is that it does not begin with the heart. A heart that is not right with God and with others may keep the law of the land, and even the letter of the law of God, but it cannot be a part of a culture of Godliness.

For that reason, the assertion of this book is that transformation begins not with culture, but with the church—the people of God. We will have limited influence on the culture as long as we start with pious proclamations about what *they* are doing wrong. We must start with understanding how *our* hearts reveal a shocking similarity to *theirs*.

For that reason, the **Culture Wars** of which I speak are not the big ticket morality/world view hot buttons that pit evangelical Christians against liberal hedonists. I am going to reference eight Cultural Indicators that reveal how much *our* hearts have in common with *theirs*. And once we identify those cultural indicators, what do we do with them? Let us now see the *Return of the Jedi* (and you thought I had forgottten about them).

Spiritual Jedi

To quote a brilliant author (ok, I'm really reminding you of what I said on the first page of the introduction), the Jedi

> *...are an ascetic group, not concerned with politics, power, prestige, or possessions. They live a life of contemplation and service. Their loyalties are not primarily political, but spiritual. They respect, support, and learn from each other. They know that their success relies on the power of The Force.*

What we need to help transform this culture are some Christians who take the Jedi approach to life from a purely Christian perspective—their spiritual loyalties, their service, their interdependence, their humility—all driven by their total surrender to Jesus Christ.

Of course, we must also point out that these spiritual Jedi know that The Force to which they surrender is the empowering presence of the Spirit of the Living God.

These things I have spoken to you while abiding with you. But the Helper, the Holy Spirit, whom the Father will send in My name, He will teach you all things, and bring to your remembrance all that I said to you. Peace I leave with you; My peace I give to you; not as the world gives do I give to you. Do not let your heart be troubled, nor let it be fearful.[7]

And did I mention their really cool light sabers?

Put on salvation as your helmet, and take the sword of the Spirit, which is the word of God.[8]

For the word of God is living and active. Sharper than any double-edged sword, it penetrates even to dividing soul and spirit, joints and marrow; it judges the thoughts and attitudes of the heart.[9]

This book is issued as a challenge. A challenge to be unsatisfied with cultural capitulation. A challenge to love God more than we love the culture. A challenge to love the culture too much to hand it over to the enemy. A challenge to become a spiritual Jedi—entering the battle for the culture, wielding the light saber of truth under the direction of the Force of God's Holy Spirit. Take the Jedi's pledge at the end of each chapter. Memorize the light saber focus so that you will be constantly ready for battle. Pray for the guiding power of the Force.

Read on, young Jedi apprentice…and may the Force be with you.

CULTURAL INDICATOR NUMBER ONE

Road Rage Culture

In the Fort Worth-Dallas Metroplex where I live (notice that I put Ft. Worth first since I happen to be one of those proud western metroplexers), there are a lot of cars. If you try to put about six million people within a few hundred square miles and then try to get all of those people to work, school, daycare, entertainment venues, etc, you are going to have some traffic.

After twenty-plus years of living in FW-D (I wonder if we can get the name of that airport changed), I've gotten somewhat accustomed to the traffic and can manage to get around pretty well. However, it is still sometimes a shock to the system of this west Texas boy who learned to drive where the space between vehicles was sometimes measured in miles rather than inches!

When I was learning to drive in the mid-1970's out in west Texas, a honk of the horn was a friendly greeting—kind of a redneck *whazzuup*! Where I live now if someone honks at you, you just got called a dirty name. Where I grew up we would wave at almost every car we met on the road. It was just so good to see someone else once in awhile. The difference between our waves back then and the waves I see often on the Metroplex freeways now is that we used to use all of our fingers!

Let me digress for a few lines here and tell you how to drive someone a little crazy when they use that unfortunate signal to tell you that you're number one. Just put on your biggest smile and wave back with the friendliest and most pleasant wave you can muster. I've done that a few times and it cracks me up to watch their response. At first they think I must be stupid, so they give me the single-digit-salute a second time to be sure I understood their intent. Then I'll just smile and wave again. Sometimes it takes two or three times, but they usually just shrug and give up and go on about their business.

Anyway…there is a term that I never heard until the past few years, but it is so prevalent now that it has actually made it into the dictionary. *Road rage*, according to Merriam-Webster Online is *"a motorist's uncontrolled anger that is usually incited by an irritating act of another motorist and is expressed in aggressive or violent behavior."*

We've all either seen personally or seen on the news the results of this aggressive or violent behavior on the roadways, but I have to tell you that I believe what happens on the road is just a snapshot of what is happening in a variety of settings across our country thousands of times every day. We have become a **Road Rage Culture**.

How is it that in America—where we have the greatest abundance of creature comforts in the entire world—we have become so angry? Many people are beginning to make that observation. An increase in the use obscene language and physical abuse toward adult authorities is widely reported among young teens and can even be found among children as young as ages five and six. Coaches and parents come to blows at Little League games before the wide eyes of their eight-year-olds. A middle-schooler's mom goes ballistic over the choir director who left her child's name off the printed program at the school concert. And speaking of music...

The best rock 'n' roll music encapsulates a certain high energy—an angriness—whether on record or onstage. Violence and energy-that's really what rock 'n' roll's all about.[10]

Oh, that must be it—that rock 'n' roll music. If we could just get everyone to sing hymns (or at least some kinder and gentler praise and worship choruses) we'd be able to soothe the savage beast of the **Road Rage Culture**.

Except it seems that those hymn-singers are not exempt from outbursts of anger. How is it that a church business meeting can turn into a red-faced shouting match over issues of eternal value like what color the fellowship hall carpet should be? How is it that an angry parent can demand that a youth minister be fired because he dared to correct an unruly teenager? How is it that a faithful church member—while purchasing supplies for the church—can publicly berate a cashier for a delay in the checkout process? (Yes, I actually witnessed that one.)

I found a couple of shocking answers to that question. It is reported that, in Africa, an outburst of rage would be considered a deep offense to many African believers because of the potential to disrupt relationships. Americans, on the other hand, don't consider anger to be that bad, especially if one is frustrated or having a bad day.[11] According to the research of the Barna Group, the religious heritage and values of most Americans has a minimal effect when it comes to moral choices.[12]

Did you get that last one? People can go to church and be taught Biblical truth. They can grow up in a "Christian home." But when it comes time to make a decision about ethical behavior, they are more inclined to reflect the culture around them than the religious teachings that have been a part of their upbringing.

What are we to do about that? As spiritual Jedi, seeking to win the **Culture Wars**, we must ask a few probing questions:

First of all, is it always sinful to be angry?

Anger is an emotional response to some sort of sensory stimulus. What that means is that we can feel anger based on something we experience with one of our senses. We see actions or hear words that violate our sensibilities. Something causes us physical pain. I suppose we could even respond in anger to something we smell or taste. The point is that we are hardwired by our Creator to be *feeling* creatures. Part of being created in the image of God is the ability to experience emotions—even the emotion of anger.

The Bible describes times when Jesus was angry.

Then Jesus went back to the synagogue, where there was a man who had a paralyzed hand. Some people were there who wanted to accuse Jesus of doing wrong; so they watched him closely to see whether he would cure the man on the Sabbath. Jesus said to the man, "Come up here to the front." Then he asked the people, "What does our Law allow us to do on the Sabbath? To help or to harm? To save a man's life or to destroy it?" But they did not say a thing. **Jesus was angry** *as he looked around at them, but at the same time he felt sorry for them, because they were so stubborn and wrong. Then he said to the man, "Stretch out your hand." He stretched it out, and it became well again. So the Pharisees left the synagogue and met at once with some members of Herod's party, and they made plans to kill Jesus.*[13]

When Jesus saw their stubborn allegiance to rules and regulations rather than compassion for a handicapped man, it made Him angry. The New Testament was originally written in Greek. The word translated *angry* in the above passage is a word that indicates an active and abiding emotional response to injustice. Was His anger sinful? If we believe that the Bible teaches that Jesus never sinned, then we must realize that it was not sinful for Him to be angry.

The Bible also describes God's anger.

*If anyone worships the beast and his image, and receives a mark on his forehead or on his hand, he also will drink of the wine of the wrath of God, which is mixed in full strength in the cup of **His anger**; and he will be tormented with fire and brimstone in the presence of the holy angels and in the presence of the Lamb.*[14]

This passage uses the same word in the original language. In futuristic and symbolic language, God's active and abiding emotional response to injustice is seen as being poured out in its fullness on those who choose to completely and eternally turn away from Him. Is that sinful? Not if we're talking about God!

The Bible furthermore teaches that it is OK for us to be angry.

BE ANGRY, AND yet DO NOT SIN; do not let the sun go down on your anger, and do not give the devil an opportunity.[15]

That's great! We have permission to be angry! When anyone tells you not to be angry, you just tell them that Ephesians 4:26 says that you can. Now before you get too excited about that prospect you better notice that the verse doesn't stop there. There are two important conditions that follow: (1) don't sin in your anger and (2) don't hold onto your anger. Oops! Have you ever violated either of those conditions? I know I have!

Well, we've established that anger is not always sinful, but we've also discovered that we haven't fully gotten a handle on the concept. I guess we need to ask our second probing question. *Is all anger appropriate?*

If the only instruction the Bible gave us about anger was what we've just read, we could be satisfied that all our anger is justifiable. But the Bible also gives us more information about anger.

*When you follow the desires of your sinful nature, your lives will produce these evil results: sexual immorality, impure thoughts, eagerness for lustful pleasure, idolatry, participation in demonic activities, **hostility**, quarreling, jealousy, **outbursts of anger**, selfish ambition, divisions, the feeling that everyone is wrong except those in your own little group, envy, drunkenness, wild parties, and other kinds of sin. Let me tell you again, as I have before, that anyone living that sort of life will not inherit the Kingdom of God.[16]*

*Get rid of all bitterness, **rage**, **anger**, harsh words, and slander, as well as all types of malicious behavior. Instead, be kind to each other, tenderhearted, forgiving one another, just as God through Christ has forgiven you.[17]*

*But now is the time to get rid of **anger**, **rage**, malicious behavior, slander, and dirty language.[18]*

*My dear brothers and sisters, be quick to listen, slow to speak, and **slow to get angry**. Your anger can never make things right in God's sight.*[19]

Now these verses, and others like them, indicate that God is not pleased with the way that anger is often expressed. Sometimes anger is expressed in Godly ways. Sometimes anger is expressed in ungodly ways.

Emotions—feelings—are not good or bad in and of themselves. They are what they are. *The question is not what you feel, but what you do with your feelings.* One of my favorite seminary professors used to say, "Feelings are wonderful companions, but terrible masters." You cannot control whether or not you have angry emotions. You can control how you express those emotions.

A spiritual Jedi knows that to give in to anger is to give in to the Dark Side. Here's the third question: *How do I know the difference between righteous anger and fleshly anger?*

Don't you just hate it when the answer to the question is another question! Does it make you mad? Just kidding! I believe we can determine our direction with some self-evaluation under the direction of the Holy Spirit (use the Force, young Jedi).

When you sense the emotion of anger rising in response to circumstances, take a moment and ask these questions:

Is my anger toward a *person* or an *action*? The Bible teaches that we are to love what God loves and hate what God hates. I grew up in church hearing the phrase *hate the sin, but love the sinner*. I'm not sure that I understood that for a long time, but at some time I finally came to the realization that God really loves people! He really, really does!

I think it was when I became a father that I came to understand that more. I love people and want the best for them. I'd do a lot of things and sacrifice a lot of things for the benefit of others. There are some people I would even die for. However, there is not one person that I would sacrifice either of my children for. You see, I don't love anyone that much. But God does. He loves everyone so much that He sent His Son to die to pay the penalty for our sins. That includes people who do evil and horrible things and don't love Him back. Jesus still died for them.

But God also really, really hates sin. He hates injustice. He hates cruelty. He hates wickedness.

When anger rises up within me—am I able to focus on wrong actions or attitudes, or am I just mad at a person? The answer to that question will help me evaluate my anger.

Another question: Is my anger motivated by *revenge* or *restoration*? What do I want to see happen to the person whose action has stirred up anger within me? Do I want to see them get what's coming to them? Do I want them to feel the same pain they have caused? Or do I want to see them changed? Do I want to see them right with God?

How we pray about circumstances sometimes reveals our heart on the matter. There's a difference between praying *for* a person and praying *at* a person. Praying *at* a person sort of says, "God, get 'em!" Praying *for* a person says, "God, change his heart. Reveal Yourself to her. Work your purpose in his life."

Still another question: What needs to change for my anger to be resolved: *me* or the *situation*? Remember Ephesians 4:26— *In your anger, don't sin. Don't hold onto your anger.* What is going to have to happen for me to move on? Will I remain angry until the situation changes? Until the person goes away? Until

I feel vindicated? Or will I choose to release my anger to God and trust Him to do His work in the situation?

I'm reminded of a story about an old donkey that fell into a deep pit. The donkey's owner tried and tried to find a way to pull him out, but the pit was just too deep and the donkey too old and too heavy. Finally the owner decided the most humane thing to do would just be to fill the pit up with dirt and bury the old donkey. So, he got a couple of people to help and they began shoveling dirt into the hole. Shovelful after shovelful, they threw dirt down into the pit onto the old donkey's back.

But that donkey wasn't interested in being buried. When a shovelful of dirt would hit him on the back, he'd shake it off on the floor of the pit and step up on the dirt. They kept shoveling and he kept shaking and stepping. After a while, the dirt was piled up high enough that he was able to step out of that pit.

When those situations come that make you feel angry will you let the situation bury you, or will you shake it off and step up out of the pit? We can't always change the situation, but we can change our approach to the situation. So if the thing that needs to change is us, that leads us to our final probing question. *How can transformation take place regarding my anger?*

Allow me to suggest three crucial elements in transforming anger and rejecting the **Road Rage Culture**.

The first element is *deliberate choice*. The plain, simple truth is that I'll be angry and stay angry until I choose not to be. If I tell my wife, my children, my coworkers, "You made me mad," then I have told them that they are in control of my emotions. If I come to the conclusion that I got angry at what they did and that I can choose to shake it off and step up out of the anger, then I have taken control of my own choices. I can get *glad* in the same pants I get *mad* in.

24

The second element is *helpless surrender*. All that talk of deliberate choice is good psychology and good theory, but it's dad-gum hard to live out (that's a good west Texas technical term). When I get cut off in traffic, when someone insults my kid, when I'm unjustly criticized—it's easy to *say* that I am in control of my emotional responses, but it's not so easy to actually *be* in control. That's when I need to fall on my face before God and admit that it's too hard for me. I need to say, "God I want to shake this off, but I can't. Please help me." I need to let the light saber of God's word reveal and cut away what is not Godly and then I need to surrender to the force of the Holy Spirit's guidance.

The third element is *willing cooperation*. It is my purpose as a spiritual Jedi, not to *use* the Force, but to *cooperate* with the Force. Jesus did not promise the presence of the Holy Spirit to help me accomplish all that I desire. He promised the presence of the Holy Spirit to help me accomplish what God desires of me.

These things I have spoken to you while abiding with you. But the Helper, the Holy Spirit, whom the Father will send in My name, He will teach you all things, and bring to your remembrance all that I said to you. Peace I leave with you; My peace I give to you; not as the world gives do I give to you. Do not let your heart be troubled, nor let it be fearful. [20] (I'll give you a hint now—you're going to see these verses a lot before you finish reading this book)

The Jedi's Pledge: I refuse to make excuses for inappropriate anger. I refuse to be baited by the anger of others. I reject the **Road Rage Culture**. I choose to love people even if I hate what some of them do.

Light Saber Focus: Ephesians 4:26-27—*"In your anger do not sin": Do not let the sun go down while you are still angry, and do not give the devil a foothold.*

Surrender to the Force: Lord Jesus, I release to You my anger. Give me strength today to live a life that demonstrates Your compassion. Amen.

CULTURAL INDICATOR NUMBER TWO

Wal-Mart Culture

From 1988—1991, I was the pastor of Trinity Baptist Church in Tucumcari, New Mexico. We had a wonderful time there with the salt-of-the-earth people who made up that little church. It was, however, quite a culture shock to move from the FW-D Metroplex (see, I'm consistent), where we had spent the previous four years, to a place I lovingly described as "in the middle of nowhere on the way to everywhere". We could do our grocery shopping locally or pick up a few odds and ends, but serious shopping required some travel. It was 110 miles east to Amarillo, 175 miles west to Albuquerque, and ninety miles southwest to Clovis. Now, you may never have heard of Clovis, but its major significance for us was that, from Tucumcari, it had the nearest Wal-Mart. That was our definition of civilization. My wife literally told women back in FW-D, "We are ninety miles from the nearest Wal-Mart!"

When I first began pondering this cultural indicator I almost didn't call it the **Wal-Mart Culture**. I remembered hearing people talk negatively about those who would buy their clothes at Wal-Mart or some other discount store. It's funny how something as simple as clothing can become a status symbol by which we evaluate people and segregate them into categories. I am tempted to write a chapter on the *I Have to Have the Right*

Label on My Jeans to Feel that I am a Person of Value Culture, but the title would have been too long. I personally care so little about the label on my clothes that I try to go to garage sales and thrift stores to find clothes that people bought at Wal-Mart and don't want anymore. One Sunday I preached a sermon entitled *Dressed for Success* and everything I had on had come from a garage sale (except my underwear—I do draw the line there).

I think it is important at this point to offer this explanation of my title for this cultural indicator. This is not intended to be disrespectful of Wal-Mart in any way. In fact, this is not even about Wal-Mart. They just happen to be the most successful example of the point I'm trying to illustrate.

People spent a lot of money on clothing and accessories in 2004. I personally was amazed when I researched the 2004 gross receipts of some of the most recognizable retailers of apparel (the places where you can get jeans with the right labels).

Gap, Inc (The Gap, Old Navy, Banana Republic)—$16.3 billion

Abercrombie & Fitch—$910 thousand

May Department Stores (Foley's, Lord & Taylor, Marshall Fields, 12 other stores)—$803 million

Dillard's Department Stores—$7.8 billion

Neiman Marcus—$3.5 billion

Then, you have the discount stores where you can get clothing, electronics, household wares, etc.

K-Mart & Sears (merged in November, 2004)—$37.1 billion

Target—$46.8 billion

Wal-Mart—$256 billion

No, that's not a misprint! With over 4500 stores worldwide, Wal-Mart was the world's number one retailer and took in more money than numbers two, three, and four *combined.* That's why they get the chapter title.

But enough about that; let me suggest some characteristics of the **Wal-Mart Culture.**

In the **Wal-Mart Culture,** *the focus is on our wants and needs.* Before we consider the needs of those around us, we make sure that our own needs are met. Now that's not necessarily a bad thing. We should take care of ourselves and make sure that our families are fed and clothed and our bills paid. Personal responsibility is an admirable quality.

The problem is that we sometimes don't know the difference between *needs* and *wants.* For the last half of the twentieth century and into the twenty-first, our culture has experienced such prosperity and has become accustomed to so many creature comforts that the line between those has been blurred. See if any of these statements sound familiar to you.

I need a new car. The old one is getting some miles on it.

I need some new clothes. The old ones are not in style.

We need a bigger house. We're cramped in the one we have.

I need some new CDs so we don't have to listen to the same ones over and over.

I need a new computer. The old one is too slow.

I need a widescreen high definition plasma TV because…well, just because.

Now, please understand me. There is nothing wrong with getting a new car, clothes, house, CDs, computer, or even a plasma TV if you can afford it. The problem is using the word *need*. It's amazing how you can need something because you saw it advertised or you walked past it in the grocery store when two minutes earlier you didn't even know you needed it!

Things that would have been considered *luxuries* a generation ago (or even a decade ago) are considered *necessities* now. I appreciate my friend Mike Bellah's book **Baby Boom Believers**[21] for bringing that reality to my consciousness a few years ago. The reality is that most of us spend a lot more time and money obtaining our *wants* than we do on meeting our *needs*. Again, there is nothing wrong with having things that you want. It does, however, explain why so many in our culture have so little to invest in benevolent pursuits.

In the **Wal-Mart Culture**, *the desire is to obtain as much as possible and spend as little as possible.* Here's why Wal-Mart is king of retailers. Falling prices. A shopping cart full of clothes for the price of a pair of designer jeans. All your household and grocery shopping needs conveniently located under one roof. In other words, more stuff in your car for less money out of your pocket and less time out of your day. The hunters and gatherers of early cultures would have really appreciated old Sam Walton. Imagine spending all day just to round up the evening meal and then having to do it again tomorrow. Boy, am I glad I got to be born into this period in history!

Once again, there is nothing wrong with being frugal. (Now, there's a good word. The next time I go to Wal-Mart, I'm going to tell someone I'm there to exercise my frugality. *Sir, you can't do that in public*). Spending within your means is a good thing. However, the axiom *you get what you pay for* did not come into usage without a strong foundation of truth.

Whether the resources are financial, time, talent, or whatever—our culture wants to obtain maximum results from minimal effort and expenditure. That explains the popularity of fad diets and "nutritional supplements". People want to lose weight without investing in a healthy lifestyle that includes consistent healthy eating habits and consistent exercise. That explains the popularity of lotteries, casino gambling, and infomercials telling us how to get-rich-quick. People want to make a lot of money without doing a lot of work. That explains the popularity of online education. People want a degree without having to spend the time and money it takes to go to classes and get an education. It also explains the popularity of self-help books. People want to find six easy steps to fix whatever problem they have without spending the time and effort necessary to break bad habits they have been developing over a lifetime. (Please continue reading books—especially this one—just don't expect your life to be transformed by a few hours of reading. Change takes time).

It's true that some things are absolutely over-priced. I have a daughter who just started college, so I'm realizing that fact in some new ways. It's also true that *cheap* and *inexpensive* are not necessarily the same thing. Similarly, *quick* and *efficient* are not necessarily the same thing. Some things in life require more investment to achieve maximum results.

In the **Wal-Mart Culture**, *the convenience is that we can take it or leave it—depending upon the desire of the moment.* Another of the secrets to Wal-Mart's success is that they put so much under one roof that we can conveniently engage in one-stop shopping. A loaf of bread and a gallon of milk for Mom…*check*…a new binder for Physics class for number one daughter…*check*…a package of socks without holes in the heel for number one son…*check*…an MP3 player for Dad (oops, I got into the *wants* instead of *needs* again). The point is that we can move up and down the aisles and through the various sections of the store and take what we want and leave what we don't want. We can pick up something not on the list because we saw it and wanted it. We can leave without something that was on the list because we decided we didn't want it after all. In fact we can even walk through the store and leave with nothing in our basket because we were just browsing (I can see it now—the latest exercise craze—Wal-Mart walking. It would certainly raise *my* heart rate, but not necessarily in an aerobic kind of way).

In our consumer oriented culture, it's great to have options. The problem arises sometimes when we want to have options in places where they are less…shall we say…optional.

I know the school has a dress code, but I want to wear what I want to wear. How dare they try to suppress my individuality!

Why should it matter whether I get to work on time? I get my work done.

Why does my husband have to know where I'm going when I go out with my girlfriends? I'm still my own person.

I don't know why we have to discuss everything. If my wife would just cut back a little each month on what she spends on groceries, we can make the payments on my bass boat.

Options are not a bad thing. Life is about making choices. But we need to understand that some choices are eliminated by other choices. The choice to take a job means that your employer has the right to eliminate some of your choices. The choice to get married means that there is another person to involve in some of your choices. The choice to have children (or the choice to engage in activity that results in children) means that there is another person to consider in some of your choices. Wal-Mart is not life because life is not always convenient.

In the **Wal-Mart Culture**, *the risk is that we will overspend on impulse and create unmanageable debt.*

Those falling prices at Wal-Mart make it possible to save so much money! Check this out—I filled up my cart for $150. All that would have cost me at least $225 somewhere else. I really didn't plan to buy that combination mosquito zapper/ card shuffler, but it was out there on the clearance rack and the price was incredible. Of course, I really couldn't afford to spend $150 this week, but I put it on my Visa. And to think, I only had coffee, hamburger meat, and raisin bran on my shopping list!

What a great deal, right? A savings of at least $75! Or was it really an impulse overspending of $125?

Here is a deeply profound statement: Wal-Mart took in $256 billion in 2004 because…are you ready for this…people spent $256 billion in Wal-Mart's stores. (I know that you are incredibly impressed with my deep thinking at this point.) All of the convenient one-stop shopping, falling prices and friendly senior citizens to greet you at the door are for the purpose of helping Wal-Mart to sell you more stuff.

That is not an evil intent. That is the American dream at its best. That is the marketplace at work. And if they can help you out by making it more convenient to get the stuff you want and making it more affordable for you, then all the better. It's a win-

win situation and I'm all for win-win situations. But is it really a win for you?

Have you ever noticed the racks of magazines, batteries, candy, nail clippers, etc that are found right beside the check out stand in almost every store you go in? Do you know why they place those items there? It is because the marketing experts know that people are more likely to buy those items as a last minute impulse. Do you know that companies pay big bucks to have their products placed on the display racks at the end of the store aisles? They are willing to do that to make their products stand out from the rest and thereby benefit from impulse purchasing. It becomes one of those situations where you didn't know you needed it until you saw it displayed.

I'm not trying to portray the retailers of the world as evil grabbers of all our cash. What I am saying is that we need personal filters and boundaries to help us spend within our means. We need to know the difference between *needs* and *wants*. We need to know the difference between using credit as a *temporary convenience* (perhaps because the establishment does not take a check) and using credit as a *delay tactic* (because I really don't have the money, but I want it right now). The fact that we *can* buy on impulse doesn't mean that we *should* buy on impulse.

In the **Wal-Mart Culture**, *the attempt is to be fulfilled by gaining stuff.* I could go on, but this chapter is getting long enough and I want to get to the bottom line. You see, all of the characteristics I have mentioned can really be boiled down to this final one. We live in a consumer-driven culture that says *he who dies with the most stuff wins.* The reality is that *he who dies with the most stuff leaves the biggest pile of stuff.* The reason people buy so much stuff is that they are attempting to be fulfilled by stuff. And since fulfillment cannot be achieved through stuff, they buy more and more with the unrealistic dream that they are just one or two items away from fulfillment.

I remember a story I heard of a business owner who was walking through his warehouse and overheard two of his employees talking. One said to the other, "I'd be perfectly happy if I could just leave here today with $100 in my pocket." The employer quickly walked over to the pair and took a crisp $100 bill from his wallet. "I've always wanted to see a perfectly happy person," he said, and handed the bill to his employee. He then turned and walked on. Before he got out of earshot, he heard his employee say, "Why in the world didn't I say $200!"

You see, if we are seeking to be fulfilled by stuff, we will never have enough stuff.

The Wal-Mart Culture comes to Church

Aren't you glad all of those characteristics are only found out there among the pagans and that the family of God is immune to such worldly pursuits? Oh no, Obi-wan, the world's empire has had far too much influence on the mindset of twenty-first century Christians. So how does that look at church? Let's examine it briefly and then talk about how we aspiring Jedi might begin to turn the tide.

Focusing on our Wants and Needs—*I'm looking for a church with...an active youth program...a vibrant children's ministry...exciting worship...an active senior adult ministry...sermons that speak to my issues...*(insert your criterion here).

Sadly, for many Christians, there is about as much prayer and seeking God's direction concerning their choice of a church home as there is concerning their choice of a grocery store. I believe that every church should seek excellence in its ministries and seek to honor God with good stewardship of resources. However, we have, to a large extent, bought into the consumer-driven mentality of our culture when we choose a church home based on what that church can offer me and my family. And once we make the choice, we are only satisfied as long as we feel that our needs and wants are being met. If that feeling changes, then we go looking for another church. *Church shopping* is the **Wal-Mart Culture** in religious garb. The spiritual Jedi understands that the focus of a follower of Jesus is not on having our needs served, but on serving as Jesus served.

> *"For even I, the Son of Man, came here not to be served but to serve others, and to give my life as a ransom for many."*[22]

Desiring Maximum Benefit for Minimal Input—There was a dear lady in our church in Tucumcari who had attended for many years and never attended anywhere else. She considered it her church home and the church considered her part of the family. Many years before, as a young girl in another city, she had trusted Christ as her Savior and been baptized to identify herself as a follower of Christ and a part of the family of God. But she would never become an official member of the church. I believe that the main reason was that she knew she would never be asked to teach a class or serve on a committee or in any other leadership capacity within the congregation as long as she was an attendee and not a member. She had tremendous energy, enthusiasm, Biblical knowledge, and good business sense. She was also very generous with her financial support. However, she had so much more of *herself* (not just her money) to offer in the service of the kingdom. I was often both frustrated and amused when we were going to be voting on an item of interest to her. She would come to me privately and say, "I know I don't have a vote because I'm not a member, but I think we should…" You see, she wanted all the benefits of membership without the responsibility of using her giftedness to its maximum effectiveness.

I have known people who regularly attended worship services and never put a dime in the collection plate. I have known people, like the lady I mentioned, who attended regularly and yet never used their gifts and abilities in ministering to others. I have known people who used to serve, but feel that they have done their duty and it is time for someone else to serve. And yet all these folks were happy to have all the benefits of church membership. And they *get* all the outward benefits of church membership. Do you know why? Because the church is not in the business of selling or bartering ministry. However, there are spiritual benefits that only come to those who invest themselves in ministering to others. The spiritual Jedi understands the *Law of the Harvest* that reminds us that reaping (picking the fruit) cannot be separated from sowing (planting the seed).

Don't be misled. Remember that you can't ignore God and get away with it. You will always reap what you sow! Those who live only to satisfy their own sinful desires will harvest the consequences of decay and death. But those who live to please the Spirit will harvest everlasting life from the Spirit. So don't get tired of doing what is good. Don't get discouraged and give up, for we will reap a harvest of blessing at the appropriate time.

Whenever we have the opportunity, we should do good to everyone, especially to our Christian brothers and sisters.[23]

Remember this—a farmer who plants only a few seeds will get a small crop. But the one who plants generously will get a generous crop. You must each make up your own mind as to how much you should give. Don't give reluctantly or in response to pressure. For God loves the person who gives cheerfully. And God will generously provide all you need. Then you will always have everything you need and plenty left over to share with others. As the Scriptures say, "Godly people give generously to the poor. Their good deeds will never be forgotten." For God is the one who gives seed to the farmer and then bread to eat. In the same way, he will give you many opportunities to do good, and he will produce a great harvest of generosity in you. Yes, you will be enriched so that you can give even more generously. And when we take your gifts to those who need them, they will break out in thanksgiving to God.[24]

Take it or Leave it / Impulse spending—I am pairing two characteristics of the **Wal-Mart Culture** here because they tend to go hand-in-hand.

One of the great benefits of my Baptist heritage is the church pot-luck lunch. I know that the story of Jesus feeding the 5,000 with one little boy's lunch is proof that there were no Baptists in that area. If there had been, a few of them would have brought a casserole just in case! Those Baptist women know how to cook. There is so much food and such a variety that even the most gluttonous person can't sample everything (You know, I never recall hearing a Baptist sermon on the sin of gluttony) and even the pickiest eater can find something to enjoy.

The pot-luck is a microcosm of church life. In most churches there are so many opportunities for service, for spiritual growth, for study, for prayer, and for fellowship that even the most ambitious and energetic person can't (and shouldn't) be involved in them all. The wide variety also provides the opportunity for even the most reserved person to find a place to plug in. The activities of the church provide a perpetual pot-luck of opportunities.

Because *church life* is like a pot-luck, some Christians mistakenly assume that the *Christian life* is a pot-luck.

I don't need to go to worship services. I can worship God as much out in nature as I can at church.

I'm so busy that I just don't have time to read the Bible and pray every day.

I'm not called to ministry. That's what we pay the church staff for.

I don't have enough money to tithe.

The list could go on. You see, the *take it or leave it* approach to Christianity results in anemic Christianity. It's a little like only doing exercise on one part of your body. (*Did you see that overweight man gasping for air from just walking across the street? Yeah, but did you see his great right bicep?*). Sounds silly doesn't it, but many people approach basic Christian disciplines the same way. (*I'll take a big helping of worship and prayer, but I'll pass on the service because my plate's getting too full.*)

The other side of the coin is the *impulse* approach to Christianity that often results in burnout and ineffectiveness (a kind of spiritual debt). There are people who will become involved in every Bible study they are invited to. Others will serve on every committee they are invited to serve on. Others feel guilty if there is a ministry of the church they are not involved in. Others give to every good cause that asks them for money. Before long, they are not completing their Bible studies or ministry tasks and they drop out. Before long, they become resentful of new ministries because of the demands on their time. Before long, they stop giving to anything because they are given out.

Time magazine has called Rick Warren one of America's most influential ministers[25] and one of America's twenty-five most influential evangelicals.[26] This is largely due to his phenomenally successful and influential book, **The Purpose Driven Life.**[27] . In it, Warren asserts five basic *life purposes* (a less threatening term than *Christian disciplines*) that answer the question posed by the book's subtitle, *What on Earth am I Here for*. Those purposes are:

Worship (giving pleasure to God)

Fellowship (participating in the family of God)

Discipleship (becoming more like Christ)

Ministry (serving God)

Mission (inviting others into relationship with God)

Powerful, profound stuff! And yet, simple and basic. The spiritual Jedi understands that the goal of Christianity is not activity for activity's sake, but focus and discipline to strengthen every area of the Christian life.

Seeking Fulfillment in Stuff—How do you measure spiritual blessings? How do you know when you have achieved God's favor? How do you know that you are getting all you are supposed to get out of your faith? Those are questions that come from a *consumer* mentality.

To be spiritual Jedi, a transformation must take place in our thinking so that we can understand this truth: God's desire is that His people would be *investors* rather than *consumers*. As long as we are focused on what we *get* out of following Jesus, we will have no impact on the **Wal-Mart Culture**.

Lord, make me an instrument of your peace.
Where there is hatred, let me sow love;
Where there is injury, pardon;
Where there is doubt, faith;
Where there is despair, hope;
Where there is darkness, light;
And where there is sadness, joy.
O Divine Master, grant that I may not so
much seek to be consoled, as to console; to
be understood, as to understand; to be loved,
as to love. For it is in giving that we receive,
it is in pardoning that we are pardoned, and
it is in dying that we are born to eternal life.[28]

Then he said to the crowd, "If any of you wants to be my follower, you must put aside your selfish ambition, shoulder your cross daily, and follow me. If you try to keep your life for yourself, you will lose it. But if you give up your life for me, you will find true life. And how do you

*benefit if you gain the whole world but lose or forfeit your
own soul in the process?"[29]*

Transforming Consumerism

How can transformation take place? Begin by *praying for
others*. As we consistently pray for the needs of others, God
will do two amazing things in our lives. The first is that He will
show us how to respond to those needs. We will have the
privilege of being partners with God and investing ourselves in
His priorities. The second is that He will show us how we have
been blessed. He'll make it clear to us that investing our
resources in His work will not result in our running out of
resources to invest. We don't invest so that we can receive and
consume. We invest so that we can receive more to invest and
be a wide open conduit of God's blessings. The best and purest
water is not found in pools, but in streams.

Secondly, we must *pray for wisdom and patience*. There are
financial, time, and talent resources that we have to use in daily
living. We need to pray for God's guidance to make the best use
of them. Some people learned in church that they should give
ten percent of their income (a tithe) to God's work because that
ten percent belongs to Him. That is partial truth. The reality is
that God owns one hundred percent. We are to be responsible
managers of all our resources. The reason some people don't
feel they can invest ten percent in God's work is that they are
not effectively managing the other ninety percent. Ask God to
show you the difference between *needs* and *wants*. Ask God to
show you the right time to invest in a *want*. If you know God has
given you the go-ahead, you can then enjoy it without guilt and
be filled with gratitude to God.

Thirdly, we need to *practice planned investment*. As we pray for God's guidance, we will not be driven by *impulse*, but by *focus*. If we tithe the first ten percent of our income, we know we must adjust our spending to fit within the ninety percent remaining. If we begin every day with investment of personal devotional time with God, we know we must adjust the activities of the day to fit within the time remaining. If we begin every week with planned investment of time and talents in public worship, discipleship, and ministry activities, then we know we must adjust the remaining activities of the week to fit within the resources remaining. A wonderful paradox is that when we operate our lives by *focus* instead of *impulse*, we will have room for impulses that come from God.

All of this comes out of intimacy with God.

These things I have spoken to you while abiding with you. But the Helper, the Holy Spirit, whom the Father will send in My name, He will teach you all things, and bring to your remembrance all that I said to you. Peace I leave with you; My peace I give to you; not as the world gives do I give to you. Do not let your heart be troubled, nor let it be fearful.[30]

The Jedi's Pledge: I refuse to focus only on myself and my family. I refuse to seek fulfillment in stuff. I reject the **Wal-Mart Culture**. I choose to be an investor in God's work rather than a consumer of His blessings.

Light Saber Focus: Luke 9:24—*For whoever wants to save his life will lose it, but whoever loses his life for me will save it.*

Surrender to the Force: Lord Jesus, I desire to give up my life for you today. Show me today how to invest all I am and have for Your glory. Amen.

CULTURAL INDICATOR NUMBER THREE

PG-13 Culture

Not long ago, my son and I made a quick trip to the Texas Hill Country to spend a couple of days tubing on the Guadalupe River and playing at Schlitterbahn, a great family water park in New Braunfels. We arrived at "the bahn" just as they opened the gates at 10:00 a.m. on a Tuesday morning. By 10:15 a.m. I came to the realization that, if the companies that make swimwear for females started setting their prices based on the amount of material they use to make a swimsuit, they couldn't sell enough of them to stay in business. It was a not-so-gentle reminder—as we tried to keep one set of fourteen-year-old eyes and one set of forty-three-year-old eyes focused where they should be—that we live in a **PG-13 Culture**.

Now, I know that some people would suggest that we live in an R-rated culture—and there are certainly places you can go where that is absolutely the case—but I think the culture as a whole is more PG-13. To give us a point of reference, let's think about the motion picture rating system.

The motion picture rating system went into effect in 1968 as a voluntary rating system to inform parents about the contents of a motion picture and the suitability for family viewing. It replaced a previous system of self-regulation of content that had been approved with the formation of the ***Motion Picture Association of America*** (MPAA) in 1922. As film-makers continued to push the envelope of "do's" and "don'ts" of film content, it became apparent that self-regulation was not the answer. So, the MPAA, in conjunction with the ***National Association of Theater Owners*** (NATO), and the ***International Film Importers & Distributors of America*** (IFIDA) introduced the voluntary rating system. It has gone through several adjustments over the years, with the PG-13 classification being adopted in 1984.[31]

There are three basic criteria that cause a film to get a PG-13 rating and I think they are good benchmarks for a discussion of the characteristics of a **PG-13 Culture**.

*In the **PG-13 Culture**, there is overt or implied sensuality.* In the world of film-making, a movie with sexually oriented nudity or depictions of sexual acts would get an R-rating. However, a partially nude person, sexual innuendo, and depictions of sexual situations (without showing of sexual acts) would result in a PG-13 rating. In other words, you can still see and hear a lot.

Am I mistaken if I suggest that all it takes is a few minutes of TV watching, radio listening, or just walking around among people to realize that our eyes and ears are taking in a lot of overt or implied sensuality? How many network television shows can go for more than two or three minutes without some reference to sex? And even if the television shows themselves don't offend, then what about the commercials? I have often gotten to the end of a commercial and honestly could not tell you what product they were advertising! It seems that sex is used to sell everything from cars to cheeseburgers.

And what about song lyrics? It's nothing new of course, but take any genre of music (country, rock, pop, etc) and you'll find than many songs contain a variety of sexual—or at least sensual—references. Tragically, it is not too hard to find some harder, R-rated sexual references in a lot of contemporary music, but most of the mainstream remains firmly PG-13.

And let's not forget about a lot of the jokes you hear. I'm not just talking about foul-mouthed stand-up comics, I'm talking about the water-cooler jokes and now the more prevalent email jokes that seem to just continue encircling the globe through cyberspace. How many email jokes do you receive that contain absolutely no sexual references or innuendo?

Now sex is not a bad thing. In fact, I consider it a very, very good thing. It's not a very, very good thing simply because it is an enjoyable physical act, but because it is a gift from a loving God intended to be experienced to its fullness within the covenant relationship of marriage between a man and woman. God invented it and intended it for pleasure as well as procreation. All the way back in the creation account of Genesis, we can find:

For this reason a man will leave his father and mother and be united to his wife, and they will become one flesh. The man and his wife were both naked and they felt no shame.[32]

They were unashamed in their nakedness because they were experiencing the fullness of their union in the way God intended. Notice that the text talks about a man and his *wife*, not a man and his *significant other*.

You can also find some fairly sensual language in the Bible. *Song of Solomon* chapter seven depicts a conversation between the bridegroom and his young bride.

(Young Man) "How beautiful are your sandaled feet, O queenly maiden. Your rounded thighs are like jewels, the work of a skilled craftsman. Your navel is as delicious as a goblet filled with wine. Your belly is lovely, like a heap of wheat set about with lilies. Your breasts are like twin fawns of a gazelle. Your neck is as stately as an ivory tower. Your eyes are like the sparkling pools in Heshbon by the gate of Bath-rabbim. Your nose is as fine as the tower of Lebanon overlooking Damascus. Your head is as majestic as Mount Carmel, and the sheen of your hair radiates royalty. A king is held captive in your queenly tresses. Oh, how delightful you are, my beloved; how pleasant for utter delight! You are tall and slim like a palm tree, and your breasts are like its clusters of dates. I said, 'I will climb up into the palm tree and take hold of its branches.' Now may your breasts be like grape clusters, and the scent of your breath like apples. May your kisses be as exciting as the best wine, smooth and sweet, flowing gently over lips and teeth."

(Young Woman) "I am my lover's, the one he desires. Come, my love, let us go out into the fields and spend the night among the wildflowers. Let us get up early and go out to the vineyards. Let us see whether the vines have budded, whether the blossoms have opened, and whether the pomegranates are in flower. And there I will give you my love. There the mandrakes give forth their fragrance, and the rarest fruits are at our doors, the new as well as old, for I have stored them up for you, my lover."[33]

Whew! That's some pretty hot stuff! (I haven't told my wife lately that her nose is like a Lebanese tower, but other than that, a lot of husbands could probably take some lessons from Solomon on words of honor, appreciation, and emotional intimacy that can open the door to the delights of physical intimacy). How great is it that God intended such a celebration of love to exist between husband and wife!

However, if you pay attention to the **PG-13 Culture**, you get the impression that the greatest hindrance to a great sex life is *marriage*. How many of the sexual situations in movies and television are depicted as being between two people who are married to each other? How many of the "love songs" specify that the singer is talking about his or her spouse?

One of the TV shows I have enjoyed is ***Everybody Loves Raymond***. There are a lot of family situations depicted that are truly funny and almost universally experienced. However, one consistent theme is the infrequency of sex between Raymond and Debora, who are married and have three children. In one memorable scene, they are discussing some of the sacrifices they have made to have a family. Debora tells Raymond that she gave up some things (like a career) to have children. She reminds Raymond that he knew he'd have to give up some things as well. He retorts, "Yes, but I didn't know it would be *sex*." The laugh track follows and the viewers get a great chuckle. Funny, yes, but another indicator that the **PG-13 Culture** sees the best sex as that which is edgy, risky, and without commitment. As a result, we use scantily clad cosmetically enhanced models to get us to buy stuff. Maybe if we buy this product, we'll get the girl, too.

*In the **PG-13 Culture**, crude or profane language is prevalent.* I'll never forget when my son—about age four at the time—went to my wife and reported that, "Dad said the *sh* word." My wife was shocked, appalled, and quite frankly a little amazed. She knew that word was not a part of my normal vocabulary and that I certainly wouldn't have exposed my little ones to such language. Fortunately for me, she chose to quiz him a little further before she dealt with me. The investigation revealed that he had heard me use the words "shut up" in a sentence. I don't know the context of my use of those two words consecutively, but he had learned the lesson well that we don't tell people to *shut up*.

His understanding of what words we do and don't use provided us with a lot of funny moments in those early years. Since he was a little guy, he loved western movies. He probably gets that from my dad. Even to this day, Zeke and his grandpa can really enjoy sitting and watching **The Western Channel**. I'll also never forget the time I walked through the room as he was watching an old John Wayne movie. I heard John Wayne use a pretty offensive phrase and immediately told Zeke that we should never, ever say that.

My wife was understandably curious when I came out of his room after putting him to bed that night. I was wearing one of those *I can't laugh out loud, but I'm about to burst* expressions. I had to report Zeke's post bedtime prayer proclamation. "Dad, I know that _____ is a very bad thing to say and I'll get in trouble if I ever say _____, so I promise I will never say _____." As I looked at his triumphant expression all I could say was, "I'm proud of you, buddy."

In the world of film-making, language gets a lot of leeway. Language that some people would consider crude is prevalent even in PG-rated films. Bathroom humor even finds its way into G-rated films. PG-13 can actually have some pretty rough language, including allowing one use of a hard sexually related word used as an expletive. PG-13 films can be filled with the name of God used as an expletive. Do you ever cringe as you hear the language used in a film marketed for family viewing? Is it necessary to have that kind of language to get people to come to a movie? Do people in the "real world" really talk that way?

When was the last time you attended a large public event such as a ball game of some kind? Even a local event on a smaller scale and with a much more controlled atmosphere—like a high school football game or a little league baseball game—can be an eye-opening and ear-stinging experience. Go to a large event like a professional game where alcohol is allowed and there is a proportionate increase in the volume and severity of the profanity used.

Unfortunately people really do talk that way in the **PG-13 Culture**. Comedians don't think they can be funny without profanity. Many people do not know how to express displeasure without profanity. The truth of James 3:5-8 is illustrated in living color every day in the **PG-13 Culture**.

Just think how large a forest can be set on fire by a tiny flame! And the tongue is like a fire. It is a world of wrong, occupying its place in our bodies and spreading evil through our whole being. It sets on fire the entire course of our existence with the fire that comes to it from hell itself. Man is able to tame and has tamed all other creatures—wild animals and birds, reptiles and fish. But no one has ever been able to tame the tongue. It is evil and uncontrollable, full of deadly poison.[34]

*In the **PG-13 Culture**, difficult situations are met with violent responses.* In the world of film-making, comic violence like a punch in the nose or a kick in a sensitive area stays firmly in the land of G or PG. Gory or graphic violence will usually garner an R. You can see a lot of fighting, weapons, explosions, blood and even death in PG-13 as long as the bodies shown remain intact.

There is a lot of violence in our culture. Certainly the news reports every day of violent situations remind us that there is much anger, cruelty, and evil in our world. However, there are a lot of angry and violent situations that never make headlines. I have already dealt somewhat with the issue of anger in the chapter on the **Road Rage Culture**, so I will be brief here.

The more I think about contemporary culture, the more I realize how many other chapters could be added to this book. One of those chapters could be about a culture of revenge. You see, we can talk a lot about violence in video games and movies and the influence that it has on our kids. We can talk about how violence begets violence and how abused children often grow up to be abusers of others. There are some people who would even tell you that spanking of children is a violent behavior that causes children to grow up and want to hit people (a philosophy with which I disagree, by the way). However, I am convinced that a lot of violent behavior is caused by an immature notion that I must get *payback* for every wrong—whether real or perceived—that I experience.

Have you ever watched two toddlers struggling over possession of a single toy? One child is blissfully enjoying the toy. The other child sees the toy, wants the toy, and does not remotely comprehend the concept of waiting for the other child's fascination with the toy to wane. So child number two takes the toy from child number one. Child number one attempts to retrieve the toy from child number two. Cries, whines, and other angry sounds emanate from both children. Without intervention, the angry sounds and struggles escalate to hitting, biting, etc while the now-ignored toy lies *un-played with* to the side.

Why is there no conversation or negotiation initiated? Why did child number two not say, "*Excuse me, but I notice that you seem to be having a whale of a good time with that toy. Would you mind allowing me a few moments to play with it at your convenience?"*

Or how about this scenario as the children are a little older:

Why did you hit Jimmy?
Because he hit me first!
Why did he hit you?
Because I pushed him.
Why did you push him?
Because he told me to shut up!
Why did he tell you to shut up?
Because I told him to shut up.
Why did you tell him to shut up?
Because he called me a bunky-head!
What's a bunky-head?
I don't know, but I didn't like it, so I told him to shut up.

Why do those things happen? Because there are three skills that we do not possess at birth and must be developed through time and maturity. One is the ability to communicate with words—to carry on a conversation. Second is the ability to understand the concept of negotiation—to share possessions and to share responsibility for handling conflict. Third is the ability to let go and not take revenge—to trust that justice will prevail.

I am convinced that much of the violent behavior that takes place in the **PG-13 Culture** is because our culture is filled with emotional toddlers walking around in adult bodies. They have never matured beyond the self-centeredness of infancy.

The PG-13 Culture comes to Church

Am I ever glad the **PG-13 Culture** is "out there" and not inside the community of faith! Isn't it wonderful that being part of a church family protects our families and keeps us firmly planted in the land of G or—in those moments when we are really living on the edge—PG. What am I saying? Is that the reality you have experienced? Not hardly!

Even children raised in Christian homes are not immune to cultural influences. According to Josh McDowell, in one three-month period, 66% of Christian kids had lied to an adult; 36% had cheated on a test; 27% had had sex; 20% had resorted to physical violence; and 8% had used illegal drugs.[35]

I don't want to spend a lot of time of details, but I'll tell you that there are very few words I've heard from the heathens at the ball games that I've not heard from Christian people. Christian people are no less likely to forward a crude email than their secular counterparts. I've seen Christian girls wear clothing to church-sponsored activities that reveal more flesh than some of my wife's lingerie! And I've seen the damage done to the family of God by angry attitudes, bitterness, unforgiveness, and hurtful words.

These are not bad people. These are not people who are not truly Christians. These are not people who really don't love Jesus. These are people who are reflecting the culture they live in and are missing the opportunity to be spiritual Jedi countering the culture with the light saber of God's truth. They are not letting the Force of God's Holy Spirit to guide them to…

An Alternative to the PG-13 Culture:

So what's a spiritual Jedi to do? With each of these characteristics of the **PG-13 Culture** we must begin today with a first step.

The first step: *Deliberate Limitation*. I have read the Bible through from cover to cover several times in my life. However, it was not until about the age of forty that I made an amazing discovery of a verse in the book of Job and a practical application of it.

I made a covenant with my eyes not to look lustfully at a girl.[36]

Job was a Godly man. It wasn't just a façade either, it was the real deal. We know it was the real deal because the Bible actually records God's words of affirmation of the depth of Job's righteousness. One of the examples of Job's righteousness was his conscious choice—in his words, *a covenant with his eyes*—not to look lustfully at a girl. A covenant is a firm commitment, a conscious agreement with understood consequences. Job understood the power of lust and how eyes that linger on the body of a girl can be the beginning of thoughts that draw our hearts away from God.

Now, we might say—knowing that the customs of Job's day are far different from ours—that it was much easier for him to make that kind of covenant. After all, women did not walk around in the kind of clothes we see in our **PG-13 Culture**. About the only thing Job was going to see uncovered in public was a young lady's face and then sometimes only partially. I want to say this as delicately as possible. *Job was a father of* *ten. He didn't need to see a woman's body exposed to know what was there.* His covenant with his eyes was not nearly so much about what passed in front of his eyes as about what he allowed to linger in his heart.

Unless we sequester ourselves away as hermits, we do not have control over what passes before our eyes. We do have control over what we allow to linger in our hearts. As one philosopher said, *We can't keep the birds from flying over our heads, but we can keep them from building nests in our hair.* I had no control whatsoever on the swimwear choices of the females at the water park. That choice was not left to me. However, there were some choices I could make. One choice was not to go to a place where women are going to be exposing themselves. That is certainly an appropriate choice— sometimes a necessary choice. For example, there is a difference between taking your son to a day of playing at the water park and taking him to a hot bikini contest.

Another choice is to deliberately choose where my thoughts go. How do you control your thoughts especially when there is a lot of visual stimulation present? I discovered a wonderful practical application that I wish someone had shared with me years ago. No one told me about it, so I'm giving all the credit to God for inspiring it. I share it with you as a gift from God.

As a normal red-blooded male, I can appreciate an attractive female without lust. In fact I often walk around in public saying things like, *"Behold, what an attractive female!"* Ok, I'm just kidding about that. God hardwired into the male design a propensity toward visual stimulation. It's not a bad thing to notice that a person of the opposite sex is attractive. However, if I start pondering the quality of her suntan, the length of her shorts, the swivel of her hips, etc (we won't even talk about the etc) I have moved into the land of lust. And it can happen so quickly—especially in the summer in Texas.

When God began to use this verse from Job to refine my thought life, I became acutely aware of how quickly normal and innocent appreciation of what passes before my eyes can turn to lustful thoughts that linger in my heart. So I began a practice— when I sense that my thoughts are beginning to turn—of praying for my wife. I thank the Lord for the gift that she has been to me. I thank Him that she is such an awesome wife and mom. I thank Him that she satisfies me fully as a lover, a partner, a companion, and a friend. I ask Him for the grace to satisfy her in all those same ways. She gets prayed for in a lot of different places. She got prayed for a lot during our day at the water park. *Friends, let me tell you it's really hard to ogle another woman while I'm praying for my wife.*

What I'm saying is that we have to make a choice. Pray for your spouse when the sensuality of the **PG-13 Culture** starts to draw your thoughts away from where they should be. If you are not married, pray for your future spouse. Pray that God would prepare your heart and protect you from making choices that would hamper your ability to experience full intimacy with the one you will share your life with. A covenant with your eyes will help you make good choices on what movies to watch, what music to listen to (those lustful thoughts can be stimulated by the words you hear as well), what jokes to participate in. I have pretty much stopped forwarding all emails of any kind, but I have made a firm commitment that I will not be a conduit for passing along material that might cause someone else to stumble into lust.

The principle of limitation does not just apply to sensuality, but to language as well.

If anyone thinks himself to be religious, and yet does not bridle his tongue but deceives his own heart, this man's religion is worthless.[37]

But immorality or any impurity or greed must not even be named among you, as is proper among saints; and there must be no filthiness and silly talk, or coarse jesting, which are not fitting, but rather giving of thanks.[38]

Do not let any unwholesome talk come out of your mouths, but only what is helpful for building others up according to their needs, that it may benefit those who listen.[39]

The Sovereign LORD has given me an instructed tongue, to know the word that sustains the weary.[40]

Our words have power and should be used in ways that are beneficial to others. Our words—even in casual conversation—should be words that are consistent with the faith that we profess. There may be moments in life when it is not appropriate to preach the gospel or talk *about* Jesus or Christianity. There are never times when it is not appropriate to talk *like* a Christian.

I remember a time in my early college years when I had let my language get a little lax. I was involved in church and in Christian campus activities. I was not living a sinful lifestyle. But, I was allowing my language to reflect the culture. On a particular day I was having some trouble with a copy machine. Two people walked in the door as I let loose with an expletive that would really be considered mild by most standards (firmly in PG land). I knew both these people. One was a girl who was fairly well-known to be on the wild side. Another was a graduate student who had been both a friend and mentor to me. My language got a wide eyed response from both of them. With a twinkle in her eye, she said, "I thought you were a good Christian boy." With sadness in his eyes, he said, "He used to be." Man, my heart was broken. I decided then and there to clean up my language so that there would be no confusion about the condition of my heart.

It is not enough to just avoid profanity. We need to ask ourselves if the words we are saying are words of building, healing, and encouraging. If not, it's time to change them.

The principle of limitation also applies to violence and revenge.

> *Never pay back evil for evil to anyone. Respect what is right in the sight of all men. If possible, so far as it depends on you, be at peace with all men. Never take your own revenge, beloved, but leave room for the wrath of God, for it is written, "VENGEANCE IS MINE, I WILL REPAY," says the Lord. "BUT IF YOUR ENEMY IS HUNGRY, FEED HIM, AND IF HE IS THIRSTY, GIVE HIM A DRINK; FOR IN SO DOING YOU WILL HEAP BURNING COALS ON HIS HEAD." Do not be overcome by evil, but overcome evil with good.*[41]

Part of growing up emotionally and spiritually is learning that conversation and negotiation is a better response than whacking someone over the head. And in those times when negotiation doesn't work and you have really been mistreated, it is important to deliberately limit the emotional toddler desire for revenge and trust God to take care of it. God knows you were hurt. God knows you didn't deserve it. God has not forgotten about you. Trust His timing and don't compound the problem by an immature and even sinful response.

I remember hearing a story a few years ago about a guy who was riding with a friend who was having some car trouble. This car kept stalling as they were creeping along in traffic. The passenger was just going bananas—partly because it seemed that they would never get to their destination and partly because the driver was so calm about the situation. Each time it would stall, he would just calmly restart it again. His blood pressure was not through the roof. He wasn't cursing the car. He wasn't even apologetic to his passenger. He just calmly restarted and moved forward. Finally, the car wouldn't start again.

Well, by this time, the driver in the next car in line had about all he could take. He began honking his horn. "You idiot," he yelled. "Get that piece of junk out of the way!" On and on it went. With each outburst from the rear car, the passenger in the front car sank lower and lower in the seat. The driver just kept calmly trying to start this now completely uncooperative car. What a tense situation!

Finally, this calm driver shifted into park and got out of the car and started ambling back toward the car behind him. His friend thought, *Oh boy! This is about to get ugly.* When he got back to the next car, he smiled and leaned into the window and said, "Hey, buddy, could you help me out a little here? Would you go up there and try to start my car? I'll sit back here and honk and yell and we'll see if it helps." Now that seems like a punch in the nose waiting to happen, but it didn't turn out that way. The driver in the rear car sheepishly apologized and then got out and helped him push his car over to the side. What a great application of those words, *"Don't be overcome by evil, but overcome evil with good."*

After taking the first step of deliberate limitation of cultural influences, the spiritual Jedi must make a positive choice that goes beyond the immediate moment and particular circumstances.

A Lifelong Choice: *Intentional Nourishment.*

And now, dear brothers and sisters, let me say one more thing as I close this letter. Fix your thoughts on what is true and honorable and right. Think about things that are pure and lovely and admirable. Think about things that are excellent and worthy of praise. Keep putting into practice all you learned from me and heard from me and saw me doing, and the God of peace will be with you.[42]

The spiritual Jedi knows that he or she cannot avoid conforming to the culture by simply avoiding negative influences. There must be consistent concentration and focus. There must be a continual development of skills. The Jedi must be so accustomed to the feel of the light saber in his or her hands that it becomes a natural and instinctive response to every circumstance. That's why the Apostle Paul didn't just tell the Philippians what to avoid. He told them where their concentration should be. He used a word, translated *think about,* that literally means to take an inventory or accounting. In other words, keep a constant focus on these things that are true, honorable, right, pure, lovely, admirable, excellent, and praiseworthy. Don't spend all your time thinking about the things you should avoid. Think about the things you should embrace.

If you and I will spend our time concentrating on and celebrating the blessings we have in our marriage relationships, we won't have to walk around reminding ourselves not to lust. If we will spend our time thinking about how we can bless and encourage other people with our words, we won't have to walk around reminding ourselves not to use crude or profane language. If we will spend our time thinking about how we can overcome evil with good, we won't have to walk around reminding ourselves not to be violent or vengeful.

That all sounds so simple when I type it into my word processor, but it's tough to live out in real life. That's why we need the power of the Force to help us know how to handle the light saber.

These things I have spoken to you while abiding with you. But the Helper, the Holy Spirit, whom the Father will send in My name, He will teach you all things, and bring to your remembrance all that I said to you. Peace I leave with you; My peace I give to you; not as the world gives do I give to you. Do not let your heart be troubled, nor let it be fearful.[43]

The Jedi's Pledge: I refuse to allow my standards of dress, speech, or behavior to be determined by what is popular and accepted. I reject the **PG-13 Culture**. I choose to live by a higher standard.

Light Saber Focus: Philippians 4:8—*Finally, brothers, whatever is true, whatever is noble, whatever is right, whatever is pure, whatever is lovely, whatever is admirable-if anything is excellent or praiseworthy-think about such things.*

Surrender to the Force: Lord Jesus, I desire a life of purity. Show me today how to focus my thoughts on You and to celebrate Your goodness in my life. Amen.

CULTURAL INDICATOR NUMBER FOUR

Divorce Culture

I have very few vivid memories of the first seven years of my life. My early childhood comes to me in unconnected fragments. One memory is vivid, however. I was sitting on a bed in a motel room and my dad, with eyes and voice uncharacteristically full of emotion, told me that my mom, my brother (age four), and I were going to be living with my grandparents for awhile. I wasn't completely sure what was going on, but it was obviously something significant. The next day began the car ride of five hours or so to Grandmother's. I remember asking my mom when we were going back. She said we weren't. I cried. It was 1969, I was seven, and my journey through *divorce* had begun.

I was unusual in 1969. I was the only kid in my class whose parents were divorced. In fact, I remember fighting with another kid at school who felt the need to point out in front of the other kids on the playground that my parents were divorced. I was the only kid at school who only saw his dad one weekend a month. I was the only kid at school who lived with his grandparents.

I would not have been unusual if I had been born a few years later. With the advent of the "no fault" divorce in the 1970's, more and more couples took the option to end their marriages. More and more kids found themselves living with grandparents. As of the 2000 Census count, about six million children in the United States lived in households with their grandparents or with relatives other than their parents. Of those children, 2.1 million were being raised solely by grandparents. The 2000 Census was the first to document this trend. It asked if grandparents lived with their grandchildren and if so, if they were responsible for more than half their grandchildren's care.[44] Currently, a first grader living with both of his or her birth parents might be in the minority among his or her classmates.

It is important to say here that I don't blame my parents for every difficult thing that has ever happened in my life. I am blessed to have a wonderful relationship with my parents and step-parents. I can't imagine how my life would be without any of them. God has worked in all their lives and the choices of more than thirty-five years ago have been dealt with. That doesn't mean that it was a good thing. It means that God has done a lot of healing and has brought a lot of good out of a very bad thing.

Over the years, a lot of people have had a lot of things to say about divorce and those who have been through it. Some strong opinions have been voiced on either the "evils" or "benefits" of divorce, depending upon who the speaker is. That's why I think it's really important to ask and answer two crucial questions before we go any further. First question: *What does God think about divorce?*

*"For **I hate divorce**," says the LORD, the God of Israel,*[45]

Some Pharisees came up to Jesus, testing Him, and began to question Him whether it was lawful for a man to *divorce a wife. And He answered and said to them, "What did Moses command you?" They said, "Moses permitted a man TO WRITE A CERTIFICATE OF DIVORCE AND SEND her AWAY." But Jesus said to them, "**Because of your hardness of heart** he wrote you this commandment. But from the beginning of creation, God MADE THEM MALE AND FEMALE. FOR THIS REASON A MAN SHALL LEAVE HIS FATHER AND MOTHER, AND THE TWO SHALL BECOME ONE FLESH; so they are no longer two, but one flesh. **What therefore God has joined together, let no man separate.**"[46]*

I've got to be honest. The Bible seems pretty clear that divorce breaks God's heart. "*I hate divorce*" is a pretty unambiguous statement. Jesus stated that God's plan was that marriage was intended to be an unbreakable covenant relationship with no expiration date. Divorce came about because of the hardness of the human heart.

But we can't stop there without asking question number two: *What does God think about divorced people?* The clear statement that God hates divorce should never be twisted into a legalistic and graceless relegating of divorced people to second class personhood who are on God's *blacklist*.

*For God so loved the world that he gave his only Son, so that everyone who believes in him will not perish but have eternal life. **God did not send his Son into the world to condemn it, but to save it.**[47]*

*But God demonstrates his own love for us in this: **While we were still sinners,** Christ died for us.[48]*

65

When Jesus had raised Himself up and saw no one but the woman, He said to her, "Woman, where are those accusers of yours? Has no one condemned you?" She said, "No one, Lord." And Jesus said to her, "Neither do I condemn you; **go and sin no more.** *"*[49]

God does not hate divorced people. God loves divorced people. God sent his Son to die for divorced people. God hates *sin* and the stain and pain it causes for the *sinner* He loves. The name of the sin is not what is important. God hates them all. The worth of the sinner is important. God loves us all.

A Cultural Symptom

If we are not careful, we will look at the staggering divorce statistics in our country and come to the conclusion that divorce is the cause of much of the pain and devastation of our society. While it is easy to see how that conclusion is drawn, it fails to get to the true root of the problem. We live in a **Divorce Culture.** Even people who have not experienced the end of a marriage in divorce have bought into the corruption of the culture of divorce. See if any of these statements sound familiar.

Life's too short be stuck in something that doesn't make you happy...

I just wasn't getting anything out of it...

It was time to move on...

It just wasn't working out...

I found something better...

When people make such statements, are they only talking about marriage? Of course not! A person making those statements may be talking about why she quit her job. Another person making those statements may be talking about why he left his church. You see, my friends, marriages that end in divorce are not the cause, but symptoms of something deeper in the **Divorce Culture.** So what are some characteristics of the **Divorce Culture**?

The **Divorce Culture** is a culture that *cannot keep commitments.* There was a time in our culture when agreements were sealed by words and a handshake. If a man told you he would paint your house a week from Thursday for fifty dollars, you knew that your house would get painted a week from Thursday and it would cost you fifty dollars. Not only that, he knew that when he finished the job, he would get the fifty dollars. There were no contracts necessary. People did what they said they would do.

At least that's what I'm told. I certainly don't remember such universal integrity in my lifetime and I suspect that the *good old days* were not quite as good as some folks remember. (It's kind of like the wife who can never quite live up to her husband's memory of his mom's cooking). The symptoms of the **Divorce Culture** may not have been as pronounced, but the seeds were there.

Somewhere along the way, a week from Thursday became two weeks from Tuesday and the fifty dollars was *before I noticed that I was going to have to do a little extra scraping and so I think I'm going to have to charge you fifty-eight dollars.* And on the other side, the promised fifty dollars at the end of the job *became I don't have it right now so I'll give you twenty dollars and then get the rest to you later.* As more and more handshake commitments were violated, people felt the need for written contracts that described the responsibility of both parties.

Fast forward to the twenty-first century and we have documents with page after page of legalese that even the attorneys can't fully comprehend and we have to hire attorneys to interpret the contracts written by other attorneys. Then we have to sign the contracts with a notary present to legally affirm the identities of the signers. Then we have to hire attorneys to somehow find a loophole in the signed, notarized contract so that we don't have to keep the commitment that we have now changed our minds about.

The problem is not with the contract. The problem is with a **Divorce Culture** that cannot keep commitments or promises. A promise today means that I will keep my word—as long as it suits me.

What does the **Divorce Culture** look like? Look into the eyes of a little boy whose dad promised to take him fishing today, but "had to" change the oil in the car instead. Look into the eyes of a grandmother whose family promised to visit her at the nursing home this weekend, but had "too many things to get done" around the house. Look into the eyes of a small church pastor who has heard once again that a family has "been led" to another church with more programs. Look into the eyes of a person who needs a medical procedure that the insurance company has defined as "elective". The list could go on and on because the inability to keep commitments is rampant in our culture.

It wasn't so in the *good old days*—or was it? Solomon was king over Israel and Judah from 970-930 B.C. The book of Ecclesiastes has been traditionally attributed to his authorship, although there is no mention of authorship in the book itself. Regardless, it was written a very long time ago—long before the *good old days* that most people think about.

When you make a vow to God, do not be late in paying it; for He takes no delight in fools. Pay what you vow! **It is better that you should not vow than that you should vow and not pay.** *Do not let your speech cause you to sin and do not say in the presence of the messenger of God that it was a mistake. Why should God be angry on account of your voice and destroy the work of your hands?*[50]

Three things stand out for me in that brief passage of Scripture. The first is that keeping of commitments is not something that we have only recently had trouble with. The **Divorce Culture** did not explode into existence overnight. It has resulted from generations of eroding integrity. A little trickle of compromise has washed away the foundations of integrity until we have a rushing river through *Promise Breaker Canyon.*

Secondly, the passage teaches that it is better not to make a promise in the first place than to make a promise and fail to keep it. Now, you might say, "Wait a minute, Gerry. The Bible is not talking about *promises* here. It's talking about *vows.*" My answer? That is exactly the problem! Shakespeare wrote, *"What's in a name? That which we call a rose by any other word would smell as sweet."*[51]

Call it a *vow,* an *oath,* a *promise,* a *commitment*—can we really differentiate? Is there really more wiggle room in a *promise* than in a *vow*? The problem is that we often make those promises too lightly. Someone asks us to attend a meeting, participate in an activity, help with a task—the requests come all the time. "Sure," we say—without giving a single thought to whether or not we'll be able to do it. It's just easier to agree to it now and figure it out later. The problem is that they have the nerve to expect that we'll really do it! How about taking every promise we make seriously—so seriously that sometimes we risk the momentary disappointment of answering *no* to avoid the long term loss of respect that comes from *answering yes* but *delivering no*.

The third thing I notice is that sometimes those broken promises have been made to God. How many times has God touched our hearts about a particular issue—perhaps through something we heard in a sermon, or through our own reading of the Bible, or simply through the gentle tugging of His Spirit on our hearts—and we told God that something was going to change. We really intended to, didn't we? What happened to my commitment to have personal time with God every day? What happened to my commitment to consistently give a tithe of my income through my local church? What happened to my commitment to get more involved in hands-on ministry? What happened to my commitment to have regular family prayer times?

But God understands and He forgives, right? How we have cheapened the grace of God by treating His amazing grace as nothing more than permission to fail! The **Divorce Culture** has corrupted even the grace of God—which He never intended to just be available to *forgive us when we fail*, but to *empower us to succeed*. A spiritual Jedi knows that a life of integrity begins by trusting God's grace to help us keep our promises.

The **Divorce Culture** is a culture that *desires instant results.* If I had to use a single word to describe twenty-first century living—especially living close to a large metropolitan area—I think the word I would use is *convenient*. Pre-cooked and pre-packaged gourmet meals are available that we can just warm up in the microwave, so why go to all the trouble and mess of cooking? Quick oil change and lube establishments can be found every few blocks, so why go through the hassle of learning to change the oil in your car? Who writes letters anymore? Snail mail is too slow now that we have access to email. And why would you take the time to sit down at your computer and type out an email when you can *IM* (*instant message* for those of you who are *so* twentieth-century) someone from your cell phone and have a response back in moments? I think we have access to so much, so quickly and conveniently, that we have become increasingly impatient. We want what we want and we want it right now.

I am convinced that one of the reasons for the breakup of so many marriages in our culture is that we carry that desire for instant results into every corner of our lives including marriage and family life. People often enter marriage with romanticized and unrealistic expectations of what life will be like. When they were dating everyone looked nice, acted nice, smelled nice and had their priorities right (meaning each one focused their attention on making the other one happy). Then they got married and discovered all kinds of irritating habits that were previously concealed. Well, that shouldn't be too difficult. After all, we live in an instant world. We'll just point out this little character flaw and clean it right up. Yeah, right.

Well, then, if we can't get this cleared up quickly, we probably were not meant to be married to each other in the first place. Life's too short to be spinning our wheels in a relationship that's going nowhere. Let's just put an end to our misery and get on with our lives. We'll all be better off anyway.

That is one of the messages of the **Divorce Culture**, but is it confirmed by observable evidence?

Using data from the *National Survey of Family and Households*[52] (a nationally representative survey) the research team of the *Institute for American Values* studied more than five thousand married adults. More than six hundred of these individuals said their marriages were unhappy. Five years later, they were interviewed again. Some had divorced or separated and some had stayed married. Two-thirds of the unhappily married spouses who stayed married were actually *happier* five years later! Less than twenty percent of those who got divorced or separated were happy five years later.[53]

Similarly, the *Oklahoma Marriage Initiative* study found that thirty-four percent of married couples had serious trouble in their marriage. Of those that remained married, ninety-two percent said they were "glad they were still together."[54]

You see, our instant culture has robbed us of the great opportunity of experiencing the benefits of perseverance. Now, please understand that I am not talking about abusive and dangerous relationships. I have never told anyone that they should get a divorce, but I would not tell a woman who is being beaten up by her husband to just be patient and it will get better. But the fact that abusive and dangerous situations exist must not cause us to deny the reality that the majority of divorces happen because of incompatibility or irreconcilable differences.

That same impatience and inability to persevere are prevalent in many areas of life. It's easier to get another job than to work through learning to effectively work with a demanding boss. It's easier to move than to learn how to get along with the neighbors. It's easier to find a new church than to go through a time of struggle.

One of the great lessons for living that can be found in the Bible says,

*Therefore, since we have so great a cloud of witnesses surrounding us, let us also lay aside every encumbrance and the sin which so easily entangles us, and **let us run with endurance the race that is set before us,** fixing our eyes on Jesus, the author and perfecter of faith, who for the joy set before Him endured the cross, despising the shame, and has sat down at the right hand of the throne of God. For consider Him who has endured such hostility by sinners against Himself, so that you will not grow weary and lose heart.*[55]

This lesson is true in marriage in particular and life in general: life is not a *sprint*, it is a *marathon*. Those who win at life are not those who start the best or run the fastest, but those who endure until the end.

On July 6, 1984, Eva Dee Priddy won the grand prize. She got to become Mrs. Gerry Lewis. Ok, maybe that wasn't the grand prize, but it was (and still is) what we both wanted. One month later we found ourselves living in Ft. Worth, Texas where I would be entering Southwestern Baptist Theological Seminary. We had graduated from college in May. Eva did what many seminary wives do. She went to work on her *PHT* (Put Husband Through). She got a job teaching first grade at Walnut Creek Elementary School in Azle.

Being married to me brought a lot of changes into her life. She had grown up and gone to college in the town where she was born. She had been a member of the same church her entire life. She lived in the same house her whole life until she went to college and moved into the dormitory five blocks away.

Living in the dorm, she never had to cook a meal. She focused on her education, worked as a resident assistant in the dorm, and finished her bachelor's degree in three years. Then she agreed to marry me.

Four and a half months after she said "yes" to my proposal of marriage, she woke up in a house with a kitchen and no dishwasher. She had a full-time job as a first grade teacher. She had a part-time ministry as the youth minister's wife (a job that she says is *way* harder than being the pastor's wife). She was at a different church. She was six hours away from hometown and Mom. And every morning, she woke up with a man in her bed!

To top it all off, the reality of teaching first graders was nothing like the theory of education she learned in her college classes. These little people can't read, can't tie their shoes, can't open their milk cartons or ketchup packages, and sometimes can't even get their pants zipped up correctly. They can't do homework and don't have the attention span to do much of anything at school. They demanded constant attention.

During her student teaching, her supervising teacher had been *her* fourth grade teacher who had loved her all her life (she even hosted one of the wedding showers). In the real job, her supervising principal was a gruff former coach who talked to his teachers like he was coaching a bunch of high school football players. She had spent her life preparing to be a school teacher like her mom and when she finally got the job she was—in a single word—miserable.

She would come home from school exhausted, crying, frustrated—feeling inadequate and questioning whether this was what she was supposed to do with her life. I didn't have the husband thing down really well (I still don't have it down perfectly), but God allowed me to give her a wonderful gift. I told her, "Honey, I know this is where we are supposed to be. I know God provided this job for you. But, after this year, you don't have to do it anymore if you are still miserable." At the end of that year, she said she thought she could make it one more. She moved to fourth grade the next year and it was a better fit for her. Each year's learning and experience made the situation better. She was a teacher (part-time when our own children were not in school) for seventeen years. Interestingly, she has, for several years, been the counselor at the same school where she first started teaching. Her official job is to counsel students. Her unofficial job includes counseling teachers and staff, many of whom experience the same frustrations she had when she started teaching over twenty years ago.

My wife's success in teaching, counseling, and getting along with supervisors (that gruff principal became one of her biggest fans) was not due to a great start and a fast track to success. It was due to perseverance, humility, and a willingness to learn. That lesson would serve a lot of people well in many areas of life. A spiritual Jedi knows that the best results in life are not always instant, but sometimes must be learned through patience and perseverance.

The **Divorce Culture** *places a high priority on happiness.* All of this impatience and inability to keep commitments probably stems from a basic desire to be happy. Wanting to be happy is not a bad thing. However, when personal happiness becomes the focus of our lives, we begin to avoid situations that make us unhappy. The result is the **Divorce Culture** that thinks *I'll be happier in*: another relationship...another church...another job...another neighborhood...another car...another school. The grass is always greener on the other side of the fence.

And so we go to the other side of the fence and discover that the green grass over there still has to be mowed. And we're unhappy again. And other grass starts looking greener. And on and on it goes.

Sometimes people are able to look beyond themselves and their own happiness and so they begin to focus on making others happy. The 1925 musical **No, No Nanette** contained a song expressing that sentiment.

I wanna be happy
But I won't be happy
Till I make you happy too.[56]

Certainly a focus on the happiness of others is better than a totally self-absorbed approach to life. But, sometimes people who focus on making others happy still can't find fulfillment. Sometimes, they still move from relationship to relationship and situation to situation never feeling that they are accomplishing their purpose. They often become co-dependent persons who need to be needed.

Our church recently had a special celebration worship service after a group of our teenagers and leaders returned from a mission trip to Mexico. We saw their pictures and heard their testimonies of how God worked in and through their lives. At the end of the service, they taught us a little song that they sang with the boys and girls in Mexico.

La vida sin Cristo es como una dona. Como una dona. Como una dona. La vida sin Cristo es como una dona con un vacio en el medio del corazon. (Life without Christ is like a donut with a hole in the middle of the heart)

You have probably heard the idea that we were created with a God-shaped void in our lives that can only be filled by Him. So many people experience frustration and dissatisfaction in every relationship and situation because they are trying to find fulfillment in relationships and situations. The constant feeling of emptiness—that something is missing—is like an itch that can't be scratched. It's like trying to fit a square peg in a round hole. Nothing fits in the God-shaped void except for God. And the only way to have God in your life is by a faith relationship with Jesus Christ.

Jesus said to him, "I am the way, and the truth, and the life; no one comes to the Father but through Me.[57]

But many who have filled that God-shaped void through faith in Christ discover that there are still times when they are not perfectly happy and completely fulfilled with life's experiences. People who know Jesus Christ still can get caught up in the deception of the **Divorce Culture**. And so they keep trying to find the perfect church, the perfect house, the perfect job, and the perfect friends that make life perfect.

I suggest to you that we are not only created with a God-shaped void, but we are also created with a *heaven*-shaped void.

*Therefore if you have been raised up with Christ, keep seeking the things above, where Christ is, seated at the right hand of God. **Set your mind on the things above, not on the things that are on earth. For you have died and your life is hidden with Christ in God. When Christ, who is our life, is revealed, then you also will be revealed with Him in glory.***[58]

God created us with a hunger for heaven. If we could be perfectly happy and completely fulfilled with the imperfect and temporary things of earth, there would be no need for a place of ultimate fulfillment. If we could be perfectly happy and completely fulfilled with knowing Jesus Christ by faith, there would be no need for a place where we will one day see Him face to face. That's must be what Albert Brumley was thinking about when he wrote, *This World is Not My Home.*[59] If we try to feel completely "at home" in this world and don't realize that we are passing through, we will be continually frustrated because the reality is that our happiness and fulfillment can only be partial in this imperfect and temporary world. If we make happiness our ultimate goal, we'll never find it. The Spiritual Jedi knows that, if we make pleasing Jesus our ultimate goal, we will one day be perfectly happy and completely fulfilled in His presence.

Transforming the Divorce culture: Surrender to the Force.

These things I have spoken to you while abiding with you. But the Helper, the Holy Spirit, whom the Father will send in My name, He will teach you all things, and bring to your remembrance all that I said to you. Peace I leave with you; My peace I give to you; not as the world gives do I give to you. Do not let your heart be troubled, nor let it be fearful.[60]

The Jedi's Pledge: I refuse to be driven by what makes me feel happy. I reject the **Divorce Culture**. I choose to be driven by a desire to please Jesus Christ.

Light Saber Focus: Colossians 3:1-2—*Since, then, you have been raised with Christ, set your hearts on things above, where*

Christ is seated at the right hand of God. Set your minds on things above, not on earthly things.

Surrender to the Force: Lord Jesus, I desire a life of integrity. Show me today what commitments to make and how to keep them for Your glory. Amen.

CULTURAL INDICATOR NUMBER FIVE

Blame Game Culture

If you're ever having a bad day, just remember that you could be Steve Bartman. I imagine that when he got out of bed on the morning of October 14, 2003 he thought it was going to be a great day. A lifetime Chicago Cubs fan, he had a ticket for a box seat in the left field corner behind the bullpen at Wrigley Field, where that night his beloved Cubbies were hosting the Florida Marlins in Game Six of the National League Championship Series. The Cubs were leading the Marlins three games to two. A win that night would send them to their first World Series appearance since 1945.

By the end of the seventh inning, Wrigley was one gigantic party and Steve was living a Cub fan's dream. He had never seen the Cubs in the World Series. Their last appearance was thirty-two years before he was born! The eighth inning began with the Marlins at bat and the Cubs leading 3-0. With one out and a runner on second base, Marlin second baseman Luis Castillo hit a long fly ball that drifted foul and headed for the box where Steve was now standing in celebration. What a dream of every fan! To catch a foul ball at a Major League game—and not just any game, but the game where your team clinches a ticket to the Big Dance! Eyes glued to the ball, Steve reached out for it, never noticing that Cubs left fielder Moises Alou was charging toward the wall to attempt a leaping "highlight-reel" catch.

The next few seconds changed Steve Bartman's life. He didn't make the catch. Neither did Moises Alou, who slammed his glove to the ground in anger. The Cubs pled for a call of fan interference, but video replay clearly showed that—while Alou had a legitimate chance to catch the ball—the ball was landing in the seating area and not on the field of play. By the time the Marlins had scored eight runs in their half of the eighth inning to take an 8-3 lead, Steve was no longer at the ball park. He left with a police escort, his head covered by a jacket to protect him from all the beer being thrown at him. Instead of hearing cheers directed toward his beloved Cubs, he heard chants of "Kill him!" and "He cost us the World Series!"

According to The Wall Street Journal, Bartman's name, as well as personal information about him, appeared on Major League Baseball's online message boards minutes after the game ended. The next day, the Chicago Sun-Times also released his name, as well as his address and place of business, in an online article; the editor justified this by saying Bartman's information was already "out there". Bartman was hounded by reporters; he had his phone disconnected, and did not go to work.[61]

Steve Bartman will be forever known as *the fan that cost the Cubs their trip to the World Series*. Of course, it was the nine Cubs who were *on the field* that could not get two more Marlins out before eight runs scored. It was Cubs shortstop Alex Gonzalez who fumbled a routine ground ball that should have been an easy double play to end the inning when the score was 3-1 in favor of the Cubs. But Steve gets the blame in a culture that needs a scapegoat. Poor Steve. He's the poster child for the **Blame Game Culture.**

What does the **Blame Game Culture** look like? I'm glad you asked.

In the **Blame Game Culture** there is a *passionate need to assign accountability.* It is not enough to determine what happened or even why it happened—someone has got to be blamed. It's somebody's fault! Who did this? We cannot move forward with life until we have determined who is to blame. If we cannot determine who is to blame, we'll blame somebody anyway. Like school kids on the playground, we've become a society of tattle-tales.

You started it!
Uh-uh, you started it!
It's your fault!
I'm telling!

In the **Blame Game Culture** there is *an overemphasis on punishment and retribution.* It's not enough to find who is to blame for what happened, we also need to determine who is going to pay for what happened. It makes sense in a civilized society to have laws and to punish those who break the law. However, the **Blame Game Culture** needs to be sure that people are punished for the pain and suffering and inconvenience they have caused as well. We also want to be sure that those who experience the pain, suffering, and inconvenience are somehow compensated for it. Thus, we have a culture with a propensity toward litigation (that's sort of a sanitized way of saying that we are *sue-happy*).

Have you been injured...experienced poor workmanship...found a fly in your soup? We can help! Call 1-800-SUE-4YOU[62]

In the **Blame Game Culture** there is an *inability to release bitterness until a personal sense of justice has been satisfied.* Some things are hard to get over. Some things are impossible to forget. But, in the **Blame Game Culture**, we often hold on to hurts until we feel that the guilty party has been adequately punished. It's not enough to find out who is to blame for what happened or even to find out who is going to pay for what happened, we have to be sure they pay *enough* for what happened.

Counselors tell us some interesting facts about the grief process. A man dies when his car is hit by a drunk driver. His family is devastated. They will experience a variety of expressions of grief (shock, despair, anger, depression) for months. While the drunk driver is on trial for intoxication manslaughter, their grieving lingers. Once he is convicted and sentenced, they begin to talk about closure. They begin to talk about moving on with their lives. But an interesting thing happens if there is also litigation involved. The grief process is extended. The bitterness lingers. Closure is delayed. As long as we don't believe someone has paid quite enough, we refuse to release it.

These first three characteristics are—to a great extent—reactionary in nature. They may result from frustration over what I consider the *bottom line* characteristic: in the **Blame Game Culture** there is an *alarming avoidance of personal responsibility.* Our tattle-tale culture has a passionate need to assign blame—magnifying the most miniscule failures of others—because we have become a culture of excuse-makers when it comes to our own actions.

On November 27, 1978, Dan White, a former San Francisco city supervisor who had recently resigned his position, entered San Francisco City Hall through a basement window and shot and killed mayor George Moscone and supervisor Harvey Milk. Following his subsequent trial for these murders, a new term was added to the lexicon of our culture—you've probably heard of it—the *Twinkie Defense*. The *Twinkie Defense* came to represent excuses made by criminals to explain that external forces beyond their control caused them to act the way they did.

Contrary to popular mythology, Dan White's defense team did *not* assert that the sugar in Twinkies and soft drinks *caused* a diminished capacity for understanding right and wrong. However, psychologist Dr. Martin Blinder testified as an expert witness for the defense that the formerly health-conscious White's recent diet of Twinkies and other junk food was *evidence* that he was suffering from depression and therefore was operating in a diminished capacity. White was judged incapable of premeditation and was convicted of the lesser crime of voluntary manslaughter. The Twinkies didn't make him do it, but the Twinkies were offered as evidence that the depression made him do it.[63]

The *Twinkie Defense* is not found exclusively in the courtroom. Our culture is saturated with it and its close cousins. The *Big Mac Defense*—fast-food restaurants are making people fat, yet people won't take responsibility for their eating habits. The *Joe Camel Defense*—tobacco companies are destroying people's health, yet people who know the dangers of smoking continue to do it. The *Oreo Cookie Defense*—high-fat snack foods with slick advertisements are causing overweight and unhealthy children, yet we don't monitor their snacking and send them outside to play. The *Play Station Defense*—video games are causing violent behavior in our young people, yet we let them watch and play whatever they want.

Let's not forget the ever-popular *It's My Parents' Fault Defense*—I act this way because...*my parents were abusive...my parents were overprotective...my parents were too strict...my parents were too lenient...my parents were never there...my parents never gave me any space.*

Or what about the excuses given why people don't go to church...*there are too many hypocrites there...someone hurt my feelings...my parents made me go when I was a child and it turned me off...all they ever talk about is money.*

It would be so incredibly refreshing to hear a person say, I don't go to church *because I don't want to go to church.* At least they would be taking responsibility for their own decisions.

The Origin of the Blame Game Culture:

There's a trap we must avoid as we look around us and see all the excuses offered in the **Blame Game Culture**. I call it the *Signs of the Times Defense—that's just the way things are nowadays...it's this generation...what do you expect with all the junk on TV...I don't think we're in Kansas anymore, Toto.* The **Blame Game Culture** was not invented in the late twentieth century. It goes all the way back to the beginning.

Now the serpent was more crafty than any beast of the field which the LORD God had made. And he said to the woman, "Indeed, has God said, 'You shall not eat from any tree of the garden'?" The woman said to the serpent, "From the fruit of the trees of the garden we may eat; but from the fruit of the tree which is in the middle of the garden, God has said, 'You shall not eat from it or touch it, or you will die.'" The serpent said to the woman, "You surely will not die! For God knows that in the day you eat from it your eyes will be opened, and you will be like God, knowing good and evil." When the woman saw that the tree was good for food, and that it was a delight to the eyes, and that the tree was desirable to make one wise, she took from its fruit and ate; and she gave also to her husband with her, and he ate. Then the eyes of both of them were opened, and they knew that they were naked; and they sewed fig leaves together and made themselves loin coverings. They heard the sound of the LORD God walking in the garden in the cool of the day, and the man and his wife hid themselves from the presence of the LORD God among the trees of the garden. Then the LORD God called to the man, and said to him, "Where are you?" He said, "I heard the sound of You in the garden, and I was afraid because I was naked; so I hid myself." And He said, "Who told you that you were naked? Have you eaten from the tree of which I commanded you not to eat?" The man said, "The woman whom You gave to be with me, she gave me from the tree, and I ate." Then the LORD God said to the woman, "What is this you have done?" And the woman said, "The serpent deceived me, and I ate."[64]

Did you see that? When we left the first couple at the end of *Genesis chapter two*, we left them naked and unashamed.[65] They were in a perfect place with all their needs supplied and only one prohibition—*don't eat from the tree in the middle of the garden.*[66] Not a bad gig if you can get it. They got it and they promptly blew it! The first temptation came along and they caved in.

Now we can argue a lot of points of theology here. Why did God put that tree there and then tell them they couldn't eat from it? Why not keep them safe from it? If God knows everything then surely He knew they were going to eat from it, therefore He must have wanted them to eat from it. Why does God allow temptation? Can they really be held responsible? And how can a snake talk anyway? And on and on it goes as people ponder these eternal enigmas.

This answer may seem simplistic, but the simple truth is that God did not create *automatons* that would do His bidding because they were hard-wired to do it. God wanted—and still wants—*people* to have relationship with Him and to choose to obey Him because of that relationship. With freedom to choose comes responsibility to choose wisely.

Adam and Eve chose poorly—as we often do. But I want you to see what they did. It's the conception of the **Blame Game Culture**. When confronted with their failure and disobedience they pointed the finger at someone else! Eve blamed the snake. Adam blamed Eve. That's not the only person Adam blamed. Adam blamed God. *"The woman whom You gave to me, she gave me from the tree, and I ate."* Now why would Adam identify her as *the woman whom You gave to me.* Is that so God would know which woman he was talking about? No, Adam was saying that God shouldn't hold him accountable because it wouldn't have happened if God hadn't given her to him in the first place.

Little Billy gets caught with his hand in the cookie jar. Mom says, "Billy, I told you not to eat those cookies right now. They are for my friends that are coming later this evening." How ridiculous would it be for Billy to say, "It's your fault. If you hadn't made those cookies and if they hadn't smelled so good, then I wouldn't have made a bad choice." But that is what Adam did and that's what the **Blame Game Culture** does. We blame our choices on the actions of others and the existence of things that tempt us. We make *excuses* that sound like legitimate *reasons* in our own ears. A pastor friend of mine once told me the definition of an *excuse*: *the skin of a reason stuffed with lies.*

A New Perspective

What is a spiritual Jedi to do in the face of centuries of excuse making? We need our light saber of truth to give us a truly Christian perspective on the blame game. A spiritual Jedi understands that *we are ultimately responsible for our own actions and attitudes.*

> *For we must all appear before the judgment seat of Christ, that each one may receive what is due him for the things done while in the body, whether good or bad.*[67]

There are different judgments mentioned in the Bible. This one is not about going to heaven or hell. When the Apostle Paul wrote these words in *Second Corinthians*, he was writing to Christians and he included himself—*we* must all appear before the judgment seat of Christ. What that means is that we are all accountable for the choices we make. The rewards of heaven—the affirmations of our Savior—are not dependent on the things that happen to us, but on our Christ-like *response* to the things that happen to us. When I stand before Jesus I will not be able to make excuses or blame anyone else for the times I chose poorly. It won't do any good to point out to Him the severity of the temptations I faced.

> *No temptation has seized you except what is common to man. And God is faithful; he will not let you be tempted beyond what you can bear. But when you are tempted, he*

will also provide a way out so that you can stand up under it.[68]

I have often heard that verse misquoted. Someone will say when they are going through a difficult time, "Well, I know that God won't give me more than I can handle." Wrong! If we can handle it, why do we need Him? This verse is not about hard *times*, it is about hard *choices*. What God's word promises is that we will never face a temptation so severe that we have no choice but to give in. It may indeed be too hard for us, but if we will trust the Force, He will show us a way to choose wisely.

A spiritual Jedi also understands that *our aim should be what Jesus has given us to live up to, not what the culture has given us to live down to.*

Whatever you do, work at it with all your heart, as working for the Lord, not for men, since you know that you will receive an inheritance from the Lord as a reward. It is the Lord Christ you are serving. Anyone who does wrong will be repaid for his wrong, and there is no favoritism.[69]

We are often snared by the **Blame Game Culture** because we aim too low. We look around us and see what everyone else is doing. We see people putting forward just enough effort to stay out of trouble with the boss. We see people meeting the minimum requirements of the job description. And we see people passing the buck when their poor choices are revealed.

The question for us is whether we are going to live down to the culture and be satisfied with being like everyone else or if we are going to aim to please our Savior and live up to the standards to which He has called us. A spiritual Jedi doesn't just aim to please his or her supervisor or constituents. Meeting the minimum requirements of the job description may be enough to please them. A spiritual Jedi says, "I'm working for the Master of the Universe. I'm giving my all. No excuses. No passing the buck. No half-hearted service."

My wife was an outstanding school teacher (and is now an outstanding school counselor—with the awards to prove it). One of the reasons she was so successful was her approach to kids who had the reputation of being discipline problems. Anyone who has taught school or who has worked with children knows how disruptive and time consuming one or two troublemakers can be. They are like little leeches sucking all the energy out of the teacher and the life out of the class.

At the beginning of each year, the third grade teachers would get a list of the students assigned to their classrooms. Almost immediately the warnings would begin from the second grade teachers who had recently survived these precious angels.

You'll really have to keep an eye on this one…

This one steals from the other kids…

This one throws temper tantrums…

This one is ADHD and his parents won't keep him on his meds…

Some teachers would note these names and enter the year with a sense of dread. They would watch the kids with hawk-like intensity waiting for them to make their move. They would not be disappointed.

Eva took a different approach. She would make a note of the names as well. But on the first day of school, she would go to that child and put an arm around him or her. She'd say, "I'm so glad you're in my class this year. This is going to be a great year. I'm going to need you to be my special helper this year." Almost without exception, she had very little trouble from these kids. Did their personalities change? Did their parents' personalities change? Not at all. The change was their *perspective*. They were on Mrs. Lewis's team! They were special helpers! She was glad they were there! She gave them something to live up to and they wanted to make her proud.

Can I tell you something? The Master of the Universe is glad you are on His team! He has a special purpose for you that no one else can fulfill. He doesn't want you to be satisfied with just getting by. He wants you to succeed in your service to Him.

The spiritual Jedi understands that *the transforming influence of our lives is directly proportionate to our spiritual focus.*

Brothers, if someone is caught in a sin, you who are spiritual should restore him gently. But watch yourself, or you also may be tempted. Carry each other's burdens, and in this way you will fulfill the law of Christ. If anyone thinks he is something when he is nothing, he deceives himself. Each one should test his own actions. Then he can take pride in himself, without comparing himself to somebody else, for each one should carry his own load.[70]

Here's a good Jedi test: how do you respond when someone else blows it? Do you want to point out his sin to make yourself look good by comparison? Do you want her to be punished, humiliated, or disqualified from service? Or do you want to help lift others out of their failure and help them be useful again?

You see, a worldly focus casts blame. A spiritual focus seeks restoration. A worldly focus sees that there must be winners and losers. A spiritual focus sees that I win when I help others win. A worldly focus points out the faults in others. A spiritual focus looks inwardly to make sure that my own actions and attitudes are pleasing to God. As spiritual Jedi seeking cultural transformation, we must never forget where the transformation begins—with us.

> *These things I have spoken to you while abiding with you. But the Helper, the Holy Spirit, whom the Father will send in My name, He will teach you all things, and bring to your remembrance all that I said to you. Peace I leave with you; My peace I give to you; not as the world gives do I give to you. Do not let your heart be troubled, nor let it be fearful.*[1]

The Jedi's Pledge: I refuse to live my life captive to the choices of others. I reject the **Blame Game Culture**. I choose to take responsibility for my life and serve my Master.

Light Saber Focus: Colossians 3:23-24—*Whatever you do, work at it with all your heart, as working for the Lord, not for men, since you know that you will receive an inheritance from the Lord as a reward. It is the Lord Christ you are serving.*

Surrender to the Force: Lord Jesus, I live my life before you today without excuses. Show me today how to lift up those around me. Amen.

CULTURAL INDICATOR NUMBER SIX

Adrenaline Culture

I get email warnings almost on a daily basis. I'm not talking about personal warnings from people who want to force me to eat a liquid diet and make orphans of my children (those people don't tend to email). I'm talking about viruses, scams, cautions, etc. You've gotten them, too, if you use email. And they usually end the message with *forward this to every person in your address book if you care at all about the survival of the human race*. Well, I want you to know that I care a lot about the survival of the human race and if you will send me your email address I'll be sure that you get a copy of every forwarded message that comes to any of my four email addresses. Not!

What has really happened is that I have become very skeptical. To be honest, I've heard most of them before and I know that for every legitimate warning I receive, there will be at least ten hoaxes. If I get one I haven't heard before I check it out on one of the internet hoax databases. If I find out it's legitimate *I still don't forward it to every person in my address book*. I might mention it in a conversation or make an announcement at church, but I will leave the email forwarding to someone else.

I recently got a warning about deaths being caused from young people inhaling compressed air (the kind that comes in a can to dust electronic equipment, etc). I checked it out and found out that it was true. It is popular among good kids in our culture—the kind of kids who would never consider crack, cocaine, methamphetamines, heroin, or even pot—to get a buzz from inhaling a variety of everyday household products. They are cheap and they are legal. Our buzz-happy culture is incredibly creative in finding ways to get high.

One risk of buzz-seeking is that the buzz-seeker becomes addicted to the buzz. There is a sense of well-being that comes with the buzz and a sense that something is wrong when the buzz is not present. The result is a culture of addiction.

I remember hearing a few years ago that people can become addicted to adrenaline. If you remember your high school science (or if you can google "adrenaline") you know that it is a naturally occurring hormone that is secreted by the adrenal glands in response to either mental or physical stress. This release of hormones results in what is known as the *fight or flight reaction* where the body makes involuntary adjustments to either confront or escape whatever circumstances are causing the stress. These bodily adjustments may include increased heart rate, dilated pupils of the eye (to improve vision), and increased supply of blood to the muscles (to prepare the body for action).[72]

This heightened sense of preparation provides a kind of buzz to which the body becomes accustomed. Therefore, when the body is relaxed, a person may feel out of sorts and deliberately enter into another stressful situation.

I am convinced that this occurs more often than we realize in our busy society and that we have seen the evolution of an **Adrenaline Culture.**

So how do you know whether or not you've joined the Adrenaline Culture?

You may have joined the **Adrenaline Culture** *if your "to do" list grows longer with each task you finish.* I guess almost everyone has a *"to do" list.* It may be a daily list to remind us of the necessary tasks and errands we need to accomplish on a particular day (pick up dry cleaning, write a thank you note, finish a report, call Mom). It may be a lifetime list of goals and dreams (write a book, hike the Grand Canyon, go on a cruise, learn to play the piano). There is nothing at all wrong with having a *"to do" list.* There is nothing wrong with adding to the list as tasks are accomplished. The **Adrenaline Culture** has snared us when there is no sense of satisfaction with an accomplished task. Each accomplished task reminds us of three more tasks that we forgot to put on the list. Rather than celebrating what has been done, there is a sense of guilt for what has not been done.

I used to get a newsletter from a young lady who was involved in a para-church ministry where she had to raise her own financial support. Each newsletter included the things that God was teaching her. I noticed that God consistently taught her how inferior she was. He never taught her how He took pleasure in her availability to Him. He never taught her how to celebrate small victories. He only taught her how far she was from where she was supposed to be. I'm pretty sure that He would have liked to teach her some of those things, but learning requires open ears on the part of the learner. She was predisposed to hear God's admonitions, but not His affirmations. Her *"to do" list* just got longer and longer and she didn't ever feel that she was pleasing to Him if she did not live with a constant sense of urgency.

You may have joined the **Adrenaline Culture** *if the hurried-er you go, the behind-er you get.* Do you know anyone who seems to be constantly rushing and perpetually late? Do you know that person because he or she keeps staring back at you from your bathroom mirror? I think some people are always late because they wouldn't know what to do with themselves if they weren't! They put tasks off until the last minute because they have subconsciously become addicted to the increased heart rate and adrenaline rush that comes with the pressure of having to get somewhere in a hurry. Each task or appointment gets pushed back a little further until they are never on time for anything, but they feel good about themselves and feel important because they are so busy.

I have a friend and ministry colleague that I have not known to be on time for a meeting in all the years I have known him. He does a great job in everything I've observed, but he always appears to be so busy that he barely makes it from one important task to the next. It's easy to get caught up in trying to do a lot of things well rather than doing a few things exceptionally well.

You may have joined the **Adrenaline Culture** *if you don't own a watch or a telephone—they own you.* About the time I completed the fourth decade of my life I came to a startling conclusion—time flies whether you are having fun or not! The only thing spinning faster than the hands on my watch is the electric meter on my house with two teenagers and a houseful of electronic gadgetry (including dear old Dad's toys). Time rules. Our lives have become so scheduled that our watches become our taskmasters. Not only do we look at them constantly, but we have little alarms on them to remind us when it's time to go just in case we don't look at them for a few minutes.

I remember an old joke about a little Baptist boy and a little Catholic boy who decided they would go to each other's churches and find out what it was like. The little Baptist boy visited his friend's Catholic church first. He watched the priest and the congregation with great interest and frequently asked his friend what certain actions meant. His friend answered his questions and when they went home the little Baptist boy knew more about what it means to be Catholic. The next Sunday, they went to the Baptist church. After a few songs and some announcements, the preacher approached the pulpit, removed his wristwatch and laid it on the pulpit in front of him. The little Catholic boy asked his friend, "What does it mean when he does that?" "That," his friend replied, "doesn't mean a dad-gum thing."

I have been accused (in a good-natured way, of course) by members of my church of not being able to see the clock on the back wall. I tell them that I can see it, I'm just ignoring it. It is really important to know why that clock is on the back wall. Is it there to help me or to rule me? You see, a watch...a clock...a calendar...those things are supposed to be tools to help us. If we are not careful, they will be masters to rule us.

Here's one test of your **Adrenaline Culture** quotient: how does it make you feel to leave your watch at home for a day? When I have a day off or a vacation day, I try to be very intentional about not wearing a watch. That doesn't mean that I don't care what time it is. It means that my watch doesn't own me. It means that time is mine and I am free from the tyranny of a schedule. Those days are infrequent, but they are precious! We need to allow ourselves permission to relax and allow time to pass unnoticed. We need to experience time flying *because* we're having fun.

If it were not enough that we are sometimes owned by our watches, some of us are absolutely enslaved by our telephones. I haven't seen the study, so this is hearsay, but someone told me not long ago about a report they read that talked about how some teenagers actually have anxiety attacks when they are not allowed to have their cell phones for an extended period of time. I can believe it!

I saw something at church the other day that cracked me up. The youth department at our church is across the hall from my office. (That's why I don't do anything in my office that requires much concentration once people start arriving on Sundays.) Anyway, I was walking down the hallway and as I passed by the youth department I looked in the door and saw one of our high school girls talking on her cell phone. A few steps later I met another girl talking on her cell phone. They were talking to each other!

There are some great moments in sports just watching people and their cell phones. Like when one rings in a restaurant and fourteen people start patting themselves down trying to find out if it's theirs. Or when you answer a question from a stranger in a public place and discover that he has an ear bud in his ear and he wasn't talking to you.

I love the technology that allows us to be available more quickly, but if we are not careful the technology that is intended to help us will only create more pressure in our lives. Here's another test of your **Adrenaline Culture** quotient: can you let the phone ring without feeling compelled to answer every time? Can you allow the wonderful technology of answering machines and voice mail serve you and allow you to remain focused on what you are doing? Or do you answer every call you can and worry that you might have missed something important with the ones you can't? *Do you own a phone or does it own you?*

You may have joined the **Adrenaline Culture** *if you need a vacation to recover from your vacation.* What is the purpose of a vacation anyway? Is it to have some time away from your regular routine to recharge your physical, spiritual, and emotional batteries or is it your one opportunity to do as much as possible in a few days time because that's all the fun you're allowed to have this year?

We bought a travel trailer in 2001—nothing fancy, just something comfortable to sleep in and easy to pull behind a minivan. Since then, we've had some great family trips. We've been west to the Grand Canyon, north to Yellowstone, and east to the Great Smoky Mountains. We've made great memories, traveled thousands of miles, seen lots of sights, and come home exhausted. I wouldn't trade those experiences for anything. But can I let you in on a secret? The best use of that travel trailer has not been the ten day, 3000 mile trips to the great tourist destinations of North America. It's been the three day getaways to a nearby State Park where we camped, hiked, napped, read, roasted marshmallows over the campfire, and enjoyed each other's company.

I would wish for everyone the opportunity and resources to take in some of those great tourist destinations. I would wish even more for family times of easygoing and unhurried relaxation where the vacation is more about each other than it is about attractions.

You may have joined the **Adrenaline Culture** *if you are more concerned with serving God than you are with seeking God.* I got some of you with that one. You looked at those other examples and felt pretty good about yourself. But when it comes to your life of faith, you are all about *doing*. It is incredibly important to remember that God created human *beings*, not human *doings*. God created us for fellowship with Him, not just so He would have cheap labor to work His property. That doesn't mean that working and serving God is bad. Not at all! He wants us to serve Him. But He wants that service to flow out of our fellowship with Him. He wants us to serve Him because we have drawn close to Him in worship. If we focus on *seeking* God, our service will be informed by His presence and guidance in our lives. Our service will be empowered by His provision in our lives. If we focus on *serving* God, we risk doing our will in our power and then asking Him to bless that which He has not commanded or inspired.

So what's a spiritual Jedi to do? Take a few deep breaths. Inhale the presence of the Force. Take your Light Saber in your hand and learn to adjust the **Adrenaline Culture**.

Adjusting the Adrenaline Culture

First, we need to adjust our *ears*.

Meditate within your heart on your bed, and be still.[73]

How does God speak to you? Do you hear Him speak in an audible voice? Do you hear Him speak by an impression or thought He places in your mind? Do you hear Him speak through the counsel of another of His children? All those things are certainly ways God has spoken and does speak. However, I believe God most often speaks as we meditate on His word. I don't believe it is any coincidence that the Bible records sixteen times Jesus saying some variation of this phrase, "He who has an ear, let him hear."[74] To hear God speak, we have to listen. To hear God speak, we have to be quiet. An old saying says that God gave us two ears and one mouth so that we would listen twice as much as we speak. That includes our interaction with Him. We get so accustomed to the noise and busyness of the **Adrenaline Culture** that we must intentionally re-tune our ears to the still, small voice of God.

I saw a young lady—a college student—get the attention of more than 500 rowdy preteens without ever raising her voice. In a deliberately soft voice, she said, "If you can hear me, clap once." A few claps. "If you can hear me, clap twice." A few more claps. She repeated this a few times until no one was talking anymore and everyone was clapping the prescribed rhythm.

The prophet Elijah was part of an extreme, adrenaline-laced event where God's power was dramatically revealed. It was a powerful experience, but one that left Elijah drained physically, emotionally, and spiritually. He needed to hear God speak or he would be of no use to God anymore.

Now Ahab told Jezebel everything Elijah had done and how he had killed all the prophets with the sword. So Jezebel sent a messenger to Elijah to say, "May the gods deal with me, be it ever so severely, if by this time tomorrow I do not make your life like that of one of them." Elijah was afraid and ran for his life. When he came to Beersheba in Judah, he left his servant there, while he himself went a day's journey into the desert. He came to a broom tree, sat down under it and prayed that he might die. "I have had enough, LORD," he said.

"Take my life; I am no better than my ancestors." Then he lay down under the tree and fell asleep. All at once an angel touched him and said, "Get up and eat." He looked around, and there by his head was a cake of bread baked over hot coals, and a jar of water. He ate and drank and then lay down again. The angel of the LORD came back a second time and touched him and said, "Get up and eat, for the journey is too much for you." So he got up and ate and drank. Strengthened by that food, he traveled forty days and forty nights until he reached Horeb, the mountain of God. There he went into a cave and spent the night. And the word of the LORD came to him: "What are you doing here, Elijah?" He replied, "I have been very zealous for the LORD God Almighty. The Israelites have rejected your covenant, broken down your altars, and put your prophets to death with the sword. I am the only one left, and now they are trying to kill me too." The LORD said, "Go out and stand on the mountain in the presence of the LORD, for the LORD is about to pass by." Then a great and powerful wind tore the mountains apart and shattered the rocks before the LORD, but the LORD was not in the wind. After the wind there was an earthquake, but the LORD was not in the earthquake. After the earthquake came a fire, but the LORD was not in the fire. And after the fire came a gentle whisper. When Elijah heard it, he pulled his cloak over his face and went out and stood at the mouth of the cave.

Then a voice said to him, "What are you doing here, Elijah?" He replied, "I have been very zealous for the LORD God Almighty. The Israelites have rejected your covenant, broken down your altars, and put your prophets to death with the sword. I am the only one left, and now they are trying to kill me too." The LORD said to him, "Go back the way you came, and go to the Desert of Damascus. When you get there, anoint Hazael king over Aram. Also, anoint Jehu son of Nimshi king over Israel, and anoint Elisha son of Shaphat from Abel Meholah to succeed you as prophet. Jehu will put to death any who escape the sword of Hazael, and Elisha will put to death any who escape the sword of Jehu. Yet I reserve seven thousand in Israel-all whose knees have not bowed down to Baal and all whose mouths have not kissed him."[75]

God is not likely to yell over the cacophony of the **Adrenaline Culture** to get our attention. He is speaking softly. Are we listening? The spiritual Jedi who adjusts his or her ears to God will not only be aware of God's presence, but will also be reminded that other spiritual Jedi are listening to the voice of God as well.

Second, we need to adjust our pace.

Cease striving and know that I am God; I will be exalted among the nations, I will be exalted in the earth.[76]

You may be more familiar with the translation that says, "*Be still and know that I am God*." Either one works, but I really like the idea of "*Cease striving*." You see, a person might be still on the outside, but absolutely in turmoil on the inside. There are times when I allow myself to get caught up in the busyness of being a pastor, husband, and father of two teenagers. Sometimes it results in sleepless nights as I go over the next day's schedule and tasks that must be completed. But my turmoil never disturbs my wife's sleep. Why? Because I'm still on the outside. It is my mind that is striving, straining, and spinning like a gerbil in a cage and not really getting anywhere. In those seasons of life, it rarely helps to do more or go faster. Those times call for relaxation, recreation, meditation, and contemplation to get me moving at God's pace. Most of the people I know do not need to get busy doing more things. They need to get focused on God's agenda so they can effectively do what He asks.

When my children were little, they seemed to get more energy the closer to bedtime it was. They were really exhausted, but they were wound so tight that they were bundles of frenetic energy and constant motion. Sometimes, the only way to calm them was to physically pick them up and hold them tight. The squirms and struggles would continue for a few minutes while I held them close and spoke softly to them. Soon they would begin to relax and before I knew it, a little head with droopy eyelids was resting on my shoulder. They had *ceased striving* and were ready for Daddy to tuck them in bed.

That's how God wants to release us from the **Adrenaline Culture.** He wants to hold us close and speak softly to us until we cease striving and acknowledge that He is God. That means that we know that He is in control and we are not. The spiritual Jedi knows that the only right pace is God's pace.

Finally, we need to adjust our *perspective.*

Come to me, all you who are weary and burdened, and I will give you rest. Take my yoke upon you and learn from me, for I am gentle and humble in heart, and you will find rest for your souls. For my yoke is easy and my burden is light."

Do you know that some people are afraid to surrender to the Force because they believe that God is going to make them do a lot of things they don't want to do? They think they're going to have to go to church all the time or become a preacher or a missionary. They think Jesus must have meant to say, *Come to me and I will give you a job to do.*

The other misconception with what Jesus said goes to the other extreme. "*I will give you rest,*" is interpreted to mean that actively serving God is not important. Notice that He said, "*you will find rest for your souls.*" You see, it is possible to be actively moving forward on the outside and to have *ceased striving* on the inside. It is possible to *rest while you run.*

> *But those who trust in the LORD for help will find their strength renewed. They will rise on wings like eagles; they will run and not get weary; they will walk and not grow weak.*[78]

To understand how to do that, we have to understand the metaphor Jesus used in this passage. Those of us who didn't grow up in a pre-mechanized agricultural society may not understand what a yoke is. A yoke is a bow of wood by which two draft animals are bound together to pull a load. They must move together. One cannot go in the opposite direction from the other. When Jesus said, "*Take my yoke upon you and learn from me,*" He was saying that we are to be bound together with Him and to be going in His direction. When He said, "*My yoke is easy and my burden is light,*" He was reminding us that He is carrying the weight of the burden. It is like a mature draft animal—one that is more than able to handle the load by itself—being yoked together with a younger draft animal that is learning how to work in tandem. Jesus doesn't need our *help*, but He wants our *cooperation*.

Here is the Gerry paraphrase of Matthew 11:28-30: *Hey, you who are tired and burned out trying to keep up the pace of the* **Adrenaline Culture**—*come to me and let me give you some relief. Let me strap you into a safety harness so you won't run off ahead of me into the land of burnout. Let me teach you how to move in tandem with me so that you won't try to do the things that only I can do—the things I've never asked you to do. Then the things I ask you to do won't seem so overwhelming. I won't ask you to do any more than you can handle with my help.*

A spiritual Jedi understands that the only escape from the **Adrenaline Culture** is by surrendering to the Force.

These things I have spoken to you while abiding with you. But the Helper, the Holy Spirit, whom the Father will send in My name, He will teach you all things, and bring to your remembrance all that I said to you. Peace I leave with you; My peace I give to you; not as the world gives do I give to you. Do not let your heart be troubled, nor let it be fearful.[79]

The Jedi's Pledge: I refuse to equate busyness with effectiveness. I reject the **Adrenaline Culture**. I choose to seek God and cooperate with Him in my life's activities.

Light Saber Focus: Matthew 11:28-30—*Come to me, all you who are weary and burdened, and I will give you rest. Take my yoke upon you and learn from me, for I am gentle and humble in heart, and you will find rest for your souls. For my yoke is easy and my burden is light.*

Surrender to the Force: Lord Jesus, I want to cease striving and surrender to Your leadership. Show me Your agenda for my life today. Amen.

CULTURAL INDICATOR NUMBER SEVEN

Pffft! Culture

I called her Sally. Her family called her *Aunt* Sally. She never had children of her own, so she claimed her nieces and nephews as hers and their children were like her grandchildren. She had seen and done a lot in almost a century of living and I enjoyed listening to her tell about it. It never seemed strange to me, but I sometimes wondered how it made her feel to have a pastor the age of some of those grand-nieces and grand-nephews.

One of the greatest things about visiting Sally was that I never had the pressure of trying to figure out what to say. All I had to do was listen and nod once in awhile to let her know that I was paying attention. I have to admit that I didn't always really tune in on what she was saying. She weighed about as much as my left leg and she kept her little apartment pretty warm. I usually visited her in the afternoon and sometimes the temperature of her apartment, the one-sided nature of the conversation, and the time of the day combined to cause my eyelids to get pretty heavy. If she ever noticed that I missed part of the conversation (which I suspect she did) she never embarrassed me by saying so. I made that confession when I conducted her funeral service and all her family got a good chuckle out of it. They understood.

Sally told me stories that made me appreciate how easy my life has really been. Most of my Baby Boomer generation has no idea how hard our forebears worked to gain very little of material value. For us the value of hard work is what you have to show for it. For them knowing you gave your best was its own reward. For us, respect is a reward for performance. For them, respect was a currency by which you paid your way through an honorable life. Sally often reminded me of the intentional way that young people were taught to say, "Yes, ma'am" and "No, sir." The fact that she allowed me to be so familiar as to call her Sally is humbling to me even as I think about it now.

I found Sally to be right about most things. One common theme was her rueful commentary of the disrespectful tone of our culture. I could not agree more. In fact one way of describing the state of modern culture is better described with a sound effect than with a word. Since I can't communicate a sound effect on paper, I'll walk you through it. Slightly purse your lips and stick out your tongue. Now blow a burst of air through your lips. The sound you just made (and you and I both know that you did it) is the vivid trademark of the **Pffft! Culture**. My spellchecker doesn't like that word. Neither does the person watching you read this if you are reading it in a public place!

Respect is lacking in the Pffft! Culture.

American culture once understood that respect is a virtue to be demonstrated in all circumstances. To be a *respectful* person was just as important as being a *respectable* person. I'm afraid that our twenty-first century culture has evolved (or devolved) beyond that. We have become a generally disrespectful culture because our values have changed. I can think of at least three specific and crucial areas where the **Pffft! Culture** rears its nasty spitting head.

The first is *respect for authority*. In a culture where *freedom of choice* is seen as the ultimate expression of liberation, authority becomes suspect. People are more concerned with rights than with responsibilities. Authority is questioned when it interferes with a person's right to choose. Individual rights fly in the face of accountability to the community. Not many people want to live in anarchy, but most of them want order to be maintained by limiting the rights of others, not themselves. A telltale snapshot of how our culture responds to authority can be seen in how much attention people pay to highway signs.

Yield...I was here first

Speed Limit 60...I'm in a hurry

Stop...Close enough

Exit Only...I need to get in

Handicap Only...Why should they get the best parking spaces

I am not a letter to the editor kind of guy—unless it is a letter commending something. However, there have been a couple of times I have been compelled to respond to things written by other letter writers. Once was in response to a letter a few years ago where the writer decried the involvement of Christian people in a referendum regarding the sale of alcohol in a part of the county where he lived. Here's the phrase that put my fingers into action: *"Freedom of choice is supposed to be one of our unalienable rights being part of a democracy."*[80]

My response to that statement would be the same if I saw it today. Here's what I wrote then:

> *According to the Declaration of Independence, all human beings are "endowed by their Creator with certain unalienable rights" such as "life, liberty and the pursuit of happiness." I do not find "freedom of choice" mentioned. Even if it were, did not the citizens exercise their freedom of choice by voting in such a way that the wet issue failed? Or does freedom of choice mean that some citizens have the right to choose and others do not?*[81]

You see, some people are very self-centered in their desire to exercise their freedom of choice. They want what they want when they want it and how it affects those around them is irrelevant as far as they are concerned.

Unfortunately, many people are developing a self-centered, authority-free concept in the very place where respect for authority in particular and people in general should be nurtured—the home. If little Ashley doesn't want to pick up her toys, she doesn't pick up her toys. It's easier for Mom to pick them up herself than to deal with a rebellious toddler. It's also easier to buy the candy that little Eric is demanding in the store than to be humiliated by his blood-curdling wails when he doesn't get his way. It's easier to let Sierra or Brandon wear what they want, watch what they want, listen to what they want, and go where they want than to deal with a sullen adolescent.[82] You see, people often have no respect for authority because they have been taught—by default—that no one has the right to tell them what to do. Their rights to choose for themselves have been elevated above any responsibility to be accountable to the home or community in which they live.

Rights are not bad things. Rights are very, very good things. We must never forget that in the "good old days", many citizens of our country were denied some of the basic rights that others enjoyed. I'm incredibly thankful that we have rectified that injustice in our country's laws. However, rights without responsibility do not lead to *community*, but to *chaos*. The ancient indictment of the nation of Israel rings true even today.

There was no king in Israel at that time. Everyone did whatever he pleased.[83]

A second area is *respect for humanity*. When the foundation of respect for authority has been broken, a lack of respect for humans in general cannot be far behind. As one writer put it, we have gone from *enjoying people* and *using things* to *enjoying things* and *using people*.[84] If we continually question the rights of anyone else to interfere with our freedom of choice by having a position of authority, it's not much of a leap to begin questioning even *their right to exist* if their existence becomes a hindrance to our freedom to choose. People are more concerned with convenience than with civilization.

A civilized society values people and relationships and protects the defenseless against those who abuse their power to choose. Our **Pffft! Culture** has devalued those who do not provide some service, gratification, or benefit to us. In other words, we only have use for those who are *convenient* to us.

The obvious de-humanizing of the inconvenient can be seen in some of the more blatant ways of disrespecting humanity.

A baby is aborted because *it's not a good time to have a baby right now.* Apparently the timing of sex was convenient, but an unplanned pregnancy will really interfere with someone's agenda. Our **Pffft! Culture** de-humanizes a living soul by viewing him or her as a mass of tissue that can be removed with a simple outpatient surgical procedure and then proudly proclaims our goal of every child being a *wanted child.*

I must tell you—as a parent of two teenagers—children can be incredibly inconvenient! I can't always do the things I want to do when I want to do them. I don't always have money to buy the things I want. I have to go to events and meetings that I would never care anything about if my children were not somehow involved. And I would not change a thing! They are worth every moment of inconvenience, every tear that has been shed, every lost minute of sleep, every personal opportunity that I have missed.

An elderly person sits neglected in an understaffed and under funded "care" facility because *she can no longer contribute to society.* She may not have any family or her family may just be too busy to be there. In either case, our **Pffft! Culture** de-humanizes her by viewing her as a burden to be passed off on someone who doesn't have anything better to do. Wouldn't it be better for everyone else if she would just go ahead and die?

Now I am not against nursing homes or retirement facilities. I have had grandparents that have spent their final years being skillfully cared for by compassionate people in such facilities. Both my grandmother and my sister have been some of those skillful and compassionate people who care for others in such facilities. The hard truth is that many families are not able to provide the particular 24/7 care needed by their loved ones who are elderly or ill. Those same families remain intimately involved in the lives of their loved ones and provide the constant contact and family support needed to make that nursing facility a "home away from home" for as long as that loved one lives. The **Pffft! Culture** shows up when people are sent away because of what a family is *unwilling* to do rather than because of what they are *unable* to do.

A man stays up late at night viewing pornography on the internet while his lonely wife is *starving to death for intimate conversation*. The glistening bodies on his monitor are always available to him. They make no demands of him. They don't ask him to talk about his feelings or his dreams. They don't ask for a long-term commitment. When he makes love to his wife, he's not really with her. He's with the de-humanized objects of his lust that exist solely for his gratification. And in the process, he de-humanizes the real flesh and blood woman who has chosen to share her bed, her life, and her future with him. He would never **Pffft!** her to her face, but he dumps her daily for one imaginary sexual conquest after another.

I have already touched on this subject in the chapter on the **PG-13 Culture**, but it bears repeating that God's gift of sex can be perverted and misused to show incredible disrespect for humanity. When women (or men—yes, there are women who play with sex the same way) become nothing more than objects (real or imagined) to gratify the hormonal surges of self-centered convenience consumers, the **Pffft! Culture** splatters its contagious saliva all over the bystanding civilization.

Lack of respect for humanity and worship at the altar of convenience can be seen in more subtle ways as well.

How about the person who always seems to make friends with the most popular and influential people, but doesn't have time for regular folks? How about the person who only contributes to a charitable cause when donors are going to be recognized publicly? How about the person who takes advantage of people by suggesting un-needed repairs on a home or vehicle? The list could go on and on.

We have a wonderful benevolence ministry in the community where I live. This ministry has a director that works full-time hours for a less than part-time salary. Everyone else volunteers. These volunteer angels work hard sorting and organizing donated food, clothing, and household items to help people in need in the community. You would not believe how much time has been spent sorting through broken junk, dirty clothes, garage sale leftovers, and completely unusable items that have been dumped on the porch of the center after hours—simply because it was too *inconvenient* for someone to sort through their junk and bring their donations to the center during operating hours. I have personally been at the center when those precious volunteers have literally spent the first thirty minutes of the day moving piles of unusable junk just to make the front door accessible! Such "donors" de-humanize both the *people who help* and the *people who are helped* when they treat this center as nothing more than a place where castoff people get castoff possessions. They might as well give a big **"Pffft!"** as they surreptitiously leave their garbage bags under cover of darkness.

The third area where respect is lacking is *respect for God*. In reality, this is the root cause of the first two areas. If there is no respect for ultimate and absolute authority, why would we be surprised if there is no respect for human authority? If there is no respect for the Creator of the universe, why would we be surprised if there is no respect for humans created in His image? People are more concerned with choosing their own religion than with surrendering to the one true Reality.

As I write this chapter, my home state of Texas is considering a constitutional amendment that will seek to define marriage as being between husband and wife. The result of that election will be known by the time anyone reads this book. The fact that we are having a constitutional election on this issue is an example of the **Pffft! Culture's** lack of respect for God and His clear intention for marriage as stated in the Bible.

And the LORD God said, "It is not good for the man to be alone. I will make a companion who will help him." So the LORD God formed from the soil every kind of animal and bird. He brought them to Adam to see what he would call them, and Adam chose a name for each one. He gave names to all the livestock, birds, and wild animals. But still there was no companion suitable for him. So the LORD God caused Adam to fall into a deep sleep. He took one of Adam's ribs and closed up the place from which he had taken it. Then the LORD God made a woman from the rib and brought her to Adam. "At last!" Adam exclaimed. "She is part of my own flesh and bone! She will be called 'woman,' because she was taken out of a man." This explains why a man leaves his father and mother and is joined to his wife, and the two are united into one. Now, although Adam and his wife were both naked, neither of them felt any shame.[85]

Do not lie with a man as one lies with a woman; that is detestable.[86]

That is why God abandoned them to their shameful desires. Even the women turned against the natural way to have sex and instead indulged in sex with each other. And the men, instead of having normal sexual relationships with women, burned with lust for each other. Men did shameful things with other men and, as a result, suffered within themselves the penalty they so richly deserved.[87]

It is amazing to me that there are many professing Christians who don't see a problem with same-sex marriage! *If that's the way they are, shouldn't their choices be accepted?* Can you see how that statement elevates respect for individual choice above respect for the authority of God?

Does a person have the right to choose what to believe? Does a person have the right to choose what to worship? Does a person have the right to accept whatever religious or inspirational teachings are most personally appealing? The answer is a resounding *yes!* Every person absolutely has the right to choose whatever reality, religion, or lack thereof that he or she wishes. However, we don't have the right or the ability to have a consequence that is inconsistent with the choice.

The person who chooses to ignore the stop sign and causes a wreck can appeal all day long to their *freedom of choice*, but the consequence will be chosen by law enforcement authorities whether they respect those authorities or not.

The person who chooses to abort a baby can appeal all day long to the value of *every baby a wanted baby*, but the consequence is a lost life whether it is convenient or not.

The person who chooses to believe that there are no absolutes can appeal all day long—and for all eternity—to his or her right to *choose what to believe*, but God will not suspend His judgment just because a person does not believe His word.

Either there is truly one God and one ultimate absolute reality in the universe or there is not. Either the Bible is the written record of God's self-revelation or it is not. If the Bible is not true, then God is not the ultimate authority. Believe whatever you want. Give respect to whatever is convenient and brings immediate gratification. Support whatever political agenda seems most appealing. See who seems to have the most power and get on that team. And if the power and momentum seems to be shifting to something or someone else, change your allegiance.

But if the Bible is true and if God truly is the ultimate authority in the universe, the spiritual Jedi must come to an understanding of what God expects of us in terms of respect and honor.

Bible Perspective

We sometimes make the mistake of believing that honor and respect are ours to give to whomever we deem worthy. By that, we usually mean either those who have done something extraordinary to earn our respect and honor or someone with whom we have a mutually respectful relationship. But the spiritual Jedi realizes that God commands respect and honor. The scope of this book does not allow for an exhaustive listing, but here are a few examples.

We are to honor our parents. *Honor your father and your mother, so that you may live long in the land the LORD your God is giving you.*[88]

We are to honor the elderly and widowed. *Show your fear of God by standing up in the presence of elderly people and showing respect for the aged. I am the LORD.*[89] *Honor widows who are widows indeed.*[90]

We are to honor those in authority....*honor the king. Servants, be submissive to your masters with all respect, not only to those who are good and gentle, but also to those who are unreasonable.*[91]

We are to honor the community. *Honor all people, love the brotherhood,*[92]

We are to honor marriage in general and our spouses in particular. *Give honor to marriage, and remain faithful to one another in marriage.*[93] *...the wife must respect her husband.*[94] *In the same way, you husbands must give honor to your wives.*[95]

Did you happen to notice anything in those verses about this respect being optional? Do we have the right to withhold respect and honor from someone if we *really* don't think that person is worthy? Absolutely!

Hold your Wookies there, Jedi boy! Didn't you just say that respect and honor are commanded by God? Yes, I did. *Then how can you then turn around and say that we have the right to withhold honor and respect to those we deem unworthy?* I'm glad you asked. See, if you are one of those *more concerned about rights than responsibilities* types, then I have a good news/bad news answer for you. The good news is that you have the right to do whatever you choose. The bad news is that you have to live with the consequences of what you choose. You see, the Bible also teaches that failure in respect and honor brings consequences.

God does not honor those who do not honor Him. *Those who honor me I will honor, but those who despise me will be disdained.*[96]

God does not honor those who only give Him lip service. *The Lord said, "These people claim to worship me, but their words are meaningless, and their hearts are somewhere else. Their religion is nothing but human rules and traditions, which they have simply memorized. So I will startle them with one unexpected blow after another. Those who are wise will turn out to be fools, and all their cleverness will be useless.* "[97]

God does not honor those who fail to honor those in authority. *The presence of the LORD has scattered them, He will not continue to regard them; They did not honor the priests, They did not favor the elders.*[98]

God does not honor those who dishonor Him with self-centered worship. *The LORD Almighty says to the priests: "A son honors his father, and a servant respects his master. I am your father and master, but where are the honor and respect I deserve? You have despised my name! But you ask, 'How have we ever despised your name?' You have despised my name by offering defiled sacrifices on my altar. Then you ask, 'How have we defiled the sacrifices?' You defile them by saying the altar of the LORD deserves no respect. When you give blind animals as sacrifices, isn't that wrong? And isn't it wrong to offer animals that are crippled and diseased? Try giving gifts like that to your governor, and see how pleased he is!" says the LORD Almighty. "Go ahead, beg God to be merciful to you! But when you bring that kind of offering, why should he show you any favor at all?" asks the LORD Almighty.*[99]

God does not honor those who do not gratefully acknowledge Him. *For even though they knew God, they did not honor Him as God or give thanks, but they became futile in their speculations, and their foolish heart was darkened.*[100]

You may say at this point that old Gerry is confused (that happens a lot). He's talking about honoring and respecting *God*. We don't have a problem with that. It's honoring and respecting *people* that is much more difficult.

Well, I've got to tell you—if you have a problem with old Gerry at this point, you've also got a problem with old James.

But no one can tame the tongue; it is a restless evil and full of deadly poison. With it we bless our Lord and Father, and with it we curse men, who have been made in the likeness of God; from the same mouth come both blessing and cursing. My brethren, these things ought not to be this way. Does a fountain send out from the same opening both fresh and bitter water?[101]

You see, my Jedi companions, every person is worthy of respect and honor for two reasons: (1) Every person is created in the image of God; (2) Every person is a person for whom Jesus gave His life on the cross. When we fail to honor God's created order on His terms, we fail to adequately honor Him. And if we fail to adequately honor Him, we are faced with whatever consequences He deems appropriate.

Lest we come to the conclusion that behavior and character are irrelevant, we must consider one additional category of Biblical teaching. The Bible teaches that those who desire to be respected and honored should themselves be respectable and honorable.

Honor is for the wise. *The wise inherit honor, but fools he holds up to shame.*[102]

Honor is for the gracious. *A gracious woman attains honor, And ruthless men attain riches.*[103]

Honor is for the humble. *Fear of the LORD teaches a person to be wise; humility precedes honor.*[104]

Honor is for the righteous. *Whoever pursues godliness and unfailing love will find life, godliness, and honor.*[105]

Honor is for those who seek to be useful to God. *Therefore, if anyone cleanses himself from these things, he will be a vessel for honor, sanctified, useful to the Master, prepared for every good work. Now flee from youthful lusts and pursue righteousness, faith, love and peace, with those who call on the Lord from a pure heart.*[106]

Honor is for those who do not make it difficult for others to honor them. *And further, you will submit to one another out of reverence for Christ. You wives will submit to your husbands as you do to the Lord. For a husband is the head of his wife as Christ is the head of his body, the church; he gave his life to be her Savior. As the church submits to Christ, so you wives must submit to your husbands in everything. And you husbands must love your wives with the same love Christ showed the church. He gave up his life for her to make her holy and clean, washed by baptism and God's word. He did this to present her to himself as a glorious church without a spot or wrinkle or any other blemish. Instead, she will be holy and without fault. In the same way, husbands ought to love their wives as they love their own bodies. For a man is actually loving himself when he loves his wife. No one hates his own body but lovingly cares for it, just as Christ cares for his body, which is the church. And we are his body. As the Scriptures say, "A man leaves his father and mother and is joined to his wife, and the two are united into one." This is a great mystery, but it is an illustration of the way Christ and the church are one. So again I say, each man must love his wife as he loves himself, and the wife must respect her husband. Children, obey your parents because you belong to the Lord, for this is the right thing to do. "Honor your father and mother." This is the first of the Ten Commandments that ends with a promise. And this is the promise: If you honor your father and mother, "you will live a long life, full of blessing." And now a word to you fathers. Don't make your children angry by the way you treat them. Rather, bring them up with the discipline and instruction approved by the Lord.*[107]

An entire chapter—or even a book—could be written on that last point. For the purpose of transforming the **Pffft! Culture**, we'll sum it up by saying that if a man wants to be respected and honored by his wife, he shouldn't make it difficult for her. If parents want to be respected and honored by their children, they shouldn't make it difficult. In fact, I believe that the Bible teaches that the best place for learning these truths is a home with Jesus Christ as the head of authority and the center of devotion.

The transformed home is God's preferred plan for the training of spiritual Jedi. It is there that we learn the value of respect and honor. It is there that we learn how to be respectable and honorable. But it is not easy. We must surrender to the Force if we are ever going to see any transformation of the **Pffft! Culture**.

> *These things I have spoken to you while abiding with you. But the Helper, the Holy Spirit, whom the Father will send in My name, He will teach you all things, and bring to your remembrance all that I said to you. Peace I leave with you; My peace I give to you; not as the world gives do I give to you. Do not let your heart be troubled, nor let it be fearful.*[108]

The Jedi's Pledge: I refuse to dishonor God by disrespecting those for whom Christ died. I reject the **Pffft! Culture**. I choose to give respect and to live respectably.

Light Saber Focus: Ephesians 4:29—*Do not let any unwholesome talk come out of your mouths, but only what is helpful for building others up according to their needs, that it may benefit those who listen.*

Surrender to the Force: Lord Jesus, may there be nothing in my life, actions, words, or thoughts that dishonors You today. Help me to see those around me through Your eyes. In the name of Jesus I pray, Amen.

CULTURAL INDICATOR NUMBER EIGHT

King of the World Culture

If you saw the 1997 blockbuster, *Titanic*, you will probably not have any problem remembering what I call the *king of the world* scene. For the fourteen of you reading this book that did not see the movie (and for the fourteen million who saw it, but won't admit that you did), let me describe the scene to you.

Starving artist Jack Dawson (Leonardo DiCaprio) and his buddy Fabrizio DeRossi (Danny Nucci) have made it onto the transatlantic voyage of the "unsinkable" ship by virtue of having won two steerage-level tickets in a poker game. As the ship leaves the shores of Southampton on April 10, 1912 these two penniless friends climb out onto the bow of the ship and gaze at the horizon. The wind and the salt spray of the Atlantic Ocean in their faces bring an understandable euphoria as they symbolically leave behind the disappointments and bitterness of the past and head toward a new land and new life filled with promise. At the top of his lungs, Jack proclaims, "*I'm the king of the world!*"

Didn't that just make you want to cry? Ok, maybe not. I probably shouldn't quit my day job to go into the movie review business. But, I do think that particular scene in the movie presents a powerful parable of the final cultural indicator that we'll consider together: The **King of the World Culture.**

Old Jack was truly *king of the world* only in a really small world. He was king of *his* world, a world which included only the two people present on the bow of the ship. And he could only remain king in that world as long as Fabrizzio was content with that arrangement. A gentle nudge overboard could have resulted in the crowning of a new king. Meanwhile, back in the real world—the one that included other people—these were just two guys in the crowd.

The **King of the World Culture** is a distorted view of reality that results from what one of my preacher friends calls "ingrown-eyeballitis"—that is, a world that is too small because we are focused only on ourselves and we fail to consider our interaction with the rest of the inhabitants of the real world.

In fact, I would suggest to you that all of the previously considered cultural indicators can be traced back to the **King of the World Culture**. Let me show you what I mean.

The **King of the World Culture** is at the heart of the **Road Rage Culture.** When we feel justified in acting out in anger in response to the actions of others, we do so because our sense of stability has been violated. All is not right with the world from our perspective. And it is that perspective on the world—that everything is about me—that can turn a normal and natural emotional response to an inappropriate behavioral response. Remember that anger in response to injustice or danger is not sinful. It is our behavior in response to that anger that reveals the identity of the *king of the world* as we see it.

I remember taking a group of preteens to camp almost twenty years ago. By the time we arrived at the camp—less than 100 miles from home—one of the kids had already worn my patience pretty thin. And I was going to spend the next five days with these little darlings! We were unloading the van and getting everyone's luggage into our assigned cabin when I heard a scuffle break out in one side of the divided cabin. It was no surprise to me that the person at the center of the disturbance was the same one who had been at the center of most of my frustrations that day. When I confronted this behavior the precious child said, "Well, what would you do if you picked out the bed you wanted and then someone else put their suitcase on it?" I would like to report that I gently and patiently highlighted the error of such behavior and pointed out that such a *King Me* perspective on life was going to cause a lot of trouble for years to come—but that would be a lie. What really happened was that I very ungently proclaimed that if that happened to me *I would go and find another bed!*

You see, other people were rocking the child's world—a world in which *the child* was at the center. And *the child* was rocking my world as well. People will do that. People will inconvenience us, frustrate us, ignore us, and perhaps even endanger us, but we must learn to control our behavior and see ourselves as a part of a complex world rather than the center of it. You may want to slap someone silly (or the parents that brought him or her into the world), but don't do it. Take a deep breath and ask the true King of the World to guide your response.

The **King of the World Culture** is at the heart of the **Wal-Mart Culture.** When we cannot be content with what we have, we will spend precious time and energy trying to gain more stuff for ourselves rather than seeking to be a blessing to the world around us. The problem is—the world around us only exists for us as it affects us personally when we take the *King Me* approach to life.

As I write this chapter, it is less than a week until Christmas. There is, perhaps, no time of the year that results in less contentment. In a time when we celebrate the birth of the Savior of the world, nothing says it better than jewelry, video games, a new car...

Now I am not opposed to gifts, Santa, shopping, or anything else that may accompany the season. I am opposed to the idea that getting—or even giving—the perfect material gift is the way to find true contentment. In *King Me* world, Christmas is good when I get everything I want. In *King Jesus* world, Christmas is good when I recognize how much I have been blessed and how I can be a blessing to those around me. What I have to give at Christmas is not limited by my bank account. I can give of myself and make a difference to someone else.

Our church participates in a local benevolence ministry called the Community Caring Center. I mentioned it previously. For the past several weeks, the CCC has been collecting food and gifts to distribute for needy families in the community. Some people have donated items to the collection. Other people are in the process of organizing and packaging the items to be distributed. Other people will gather at 8:00 a.m. on December 23 to deliver the Christmas boxes to families. Givers and recipients will all be blessed, but I am convinced that those who seek to be a blessing to those around them are most blessed of all.

The Apostle Paul understood that reality when he shared his farewell message to his friends in Ephesus.

And now I entrust you to God and the word of his grace—his message that is able to build you up and give you an inheritance with all those he has set apart for himself. I have never coveted anyone's money or fine clothing. You know that these hands of mine have worked to pay my own way, and I have even supplied the needs of those who were with me. And I have been a constant example of how you can help the poor by working hard. You should remember the words of the Lord Jesus: "It is more blessed to give than to receive."[109]

The **King of the World Culture** is at the heart of the **PG-13 Culture.** When we continue to move the moral boundary lines of our lives in order to satisfy our passions, we reveal a *King Me* approach to life. When we were children, we often looked forward to growing up because we knew we could make choices that only adults were allowed to make. We did not see our parents' rules as protection of our innocence and training for productive citizenship, but as hindrance to our freedom. We may not have consciously put it in those terms, but the idea was there.

Hopefully, our parents did not bow to the whims of their belligerent children and we reached adulthood with a view of how our choices affect those around us and we chose boundaries for ourselves that provided for our own protection. They may not have been exactly the same boundaries as those our parents enforced, but they were built on consistent values. We understood that, once our parents were not there to make choices for our protection, we must protect ourselves— guarding our hearts and minds from those influences that would distract us from living Godly lives.

However, if we get caught up in the *King Me* lifestyle, we will let our guard down and be driven by the passions of the moment rather than by our anchoring values. We will let images pass before our eyes, let thoughts linger in our minds, let words flow out of our mouths that are both harmful to us and degrading to those around us. Oh, we'll make excuses and say we really aren't hurting anyone when we lower our personal standards of decency. But we mustn't simply try to avoid harming others—we must ask if and how our personal choices are actually helping others. In other words, we see ourselves as a part of a bigger picture, not as the center of it.

The **King of the World Culture** is at the heart of the **Divorce Culture.** When we keep commitments only as long as they are convenient, we reveal the true identity of our king. Kings make rules. Kings can change rules if they are not working out to suit the king.

If I see myself as king of my world, I will keep the commitments that are working out well for me. As for those that are *not* working out well for me...

Life's too short...

I didn't know what I was doing...

Oops, I did it again...

See you later, alligator...

If I see myself as a subject of the kingdom of Jesus Christ, then I treat my co-subjects according to His standard.

In everything, therefore, treat people the same way you want them to treat you, for this is the Law and the Prophets.[110]

How do I want to be treated? I want people to keep the commitments they make to me. I want people to be true to their word. I don't want my life to be undermined by someone else's momentary whim. Then that's how I should live toward others.

The **King of the World Culture** is at the heart of the **Blame Game Culture.** When we will not take responsibility for our own actions, we can always find someone to blame for the things that happen to us. In a *King Me* world, it's always someone else's fault. May I let you in on a secret? People will let you down. People will fail and disappoint you. People will lie to you. People will abandon and abuse you. Do you see the common denominator here? It's people! If you can just avoid people, you will be fine.

My friend, the question is not whether or not bad things are going to happen to you. The question is how you are going to respond to the bad things that happen to you. Will you spend your life looking for someone to blame and asking "Why me?" Or, will you choose to look for lessons and ask Jesus, "Where do I go from here?"

I have had opportunity to be a part of several mission trips to Mexico. On one of those trips a few years ago, I had the unique opportunity to give the ministry of friendship to a Mexican pastor whose wife was undergoing treatments for cancer. When my group was assigned to this church, we had no idea how this family was struggling with the fear, anxieties, and loneliness that can come to the family who ministers to everyone else. So often, there is no one there to minister to the minister. I really believe God sent us to this particular church so that we could encourage them. The Vacation Bible School and building construction projects were really the surface issues that got us in a position for the real ministry to this family.

On the next-to-last day of our week of ministry, the pastor and I were able to take a walk around the neighborhood and talk about his personal struggles with his wife's illness. I was blessed to be able to encourage him and pray for him, but he also reinforced a powerful lesson for me—and in so doing, he blessed me in ways that he will never know. He said, *"We have stopped asking 'why' and started asking 'what for'."* In other words—*what are we supposed to do with this?* They were not feeling sorry for themselves or looking for someone to blame. They were asking how God was going to use this as an opportunity to minister to others. When we reject the *King Me* lifestyle, we can stop looking for ways to blame and start looking for ways to bless.

The **King of the World Culture** is at the heart of the **Adrenaline Culture.** When we are so focused on the destination that we cannot experience the trip…when we can't see the hand of God in the interruptions in our agenda…when we see people as nothing more than something to help us reach our goals…*King Me* has taken over.

I have had days when my "to do" list was so long that there was no way I could get it done—and yet, I managed to accomplish it. I rushed from one task to the next and clicked off appointments with precision. I ate my lunch in the car while talking on my cell phone to prepare for the next meeting. At the end of the day I came home exhausted, but with a sense of pride in all I was able to accomplish.

I have also had days when my "to do" list was scrapped by mid-morning. A hospital visit lasted longer than I expected because the person really needed to talk. A phone call interrupted a project and turned into an unscheduled counseling session. A "coincidental" meeting at the gas pump turned into a trip to the coffee shop and more listening. Today's "to do" list became tomorrow's. At the end of the day I came home with a different kind of tired and with very little sense of *accomplishment,* but with a strange sense of *fulfillment.*

You see, the first example was all about me—*my* list, *my* appointments, *my* schedule, *my* agenda. The second example was about something bigger than me. It did not provide the adrenaline rush, but it actually nourished my soul (and soul-nourishing was not even on my list for the day).

The **King of the World Culture** is at the heart of the **Pffft! Culture.** When we honor only those persons from whom we expect to benefit—but expect everyone to respect us—*King Me* has once again reared his ugly head.

I want to use a slang word that has probably been replaced by something else in the current vernacular. That's the way I usually operate. Just about the time I figure out what one of these words means, it is already the *old* word and nobody is using it anymore. I don't know the difference between *cool* and *sweet* and if I try to keep up I think my brain will melt and run out my ears.

The word I'm thinking of is *Dis*. I don't mean *dis* way—as opposed to *dat* way—I mean the verb *dis*. Do you need me to use it in a sentence? Ok, *dis* is how it would sound (sorry, I couldn't resist).

Why did you beat him unconscious?

Because he dissed me.

Dis is short for *disrespect*. We live in a culture that demands respect. I have not yet run across a person who did not want to be respected. Some don't think they are *worthy* of respect, but they *want* to be respected nonetheless. And it bothers them when they are not respected. There's nothing wrong with wanting to be respected—unless *King Me* forgets that he should be respect*able* and respect*ful* if he wants to be respect*ed*.

Do you see how the **King of the World Culture** feeds the monster that responds to life with anger, greed, vulgarity, broken promises, excuse making, stress, and disrespect? Do you see how the world is becoming more and more self-centered and giving in to the Dark Side? At least in the church we have avoided the self-centeredness of the **King of the World Culture**. Right? Haven't we?

The King of the World Culture is alive and well at church.

How I wish that the influence of the Dark Side stopped at the front doors of our church buildings and that inside we could only find spiritual Jedi and those who are being apprenticed and discipled in the ways of the Force. I don't mean that I don't want "sinners" coming to church. God forbid! I want the church to be a place of healing, forgiveness, deliverance, restoration, and equipping. However, the greatest hindrance to that is not the world around us, but the worldliness within us. And that worldliness does not begin with actions, but with attitudes. And worldly attitudes originate with *King Me.*

That's actually the original temptation—to be my own boss, my own king, my own god.

Now the serpent was more crafty than any of the wild animals the LORD God had made. He said to the woman, "Did God really say, 'You must not eat from any tree in the garden'?" The woman said to the serpent, "We may eat fruit from the trees in the garden, but God did say, 'You must not eat fruit from the tree that is in the middle of the garden, and you must not touch it, or you will *die.'" "You will not surely die," the serpent said to the woman. "For God knows that when you eat of it your eyes will be opened, and **you will be like God**, knowing good and evil."[111]*

You see, my Jedi apprentice, the **King of the World Culture** is an affliction of the *eyes*. When we surrender to it, we forget the *outward* look. We overuse words like *me* and *my*.

*She sat in **my** pew...*

*He never picks **my** favorite songs...*

*He didn't come to visit **me**...*

*She didn't say hello to **me**...*

*Don't tell **me** how to live **my** life...*

*They're changing **my** church...*

Are those words bad or inappropriate words? No, they are incomplete words. Both Jesus and the Apostle Paul gave us complementary words to go with them.

A new commandment I give to you, that you love one another, even as I have loved you, that you also love one another. By this all men will know that you are My disciples, if you have love for one another"[112]

Be devoted to one another in brotherly love; give preference to one another in honor; not lagging behind in diligence, fervent in spirit, serving the Lord; rejoicing in hope, persevering in tribulation, devoted to prayer, contributing to the needs of the saints, practicing hospitality.[113]

Therefore encourage one another and build up one another, just as you also are doing.[114]

Did you see the words I'm talking about? Excellent! You got it—*one another*. Love *one another*—and not just any kind of love, but like Jesus loved. Isn't it amazing that Jesus said the identifying characteristic of His followers would be how they love one another—not their theological orthodoxy or missionary zeal—how they love one another!

A few years later, the Apostle Paul would help us to understand what that love looks like. Be devoted to *one another*. Give preference to *one another*. Contribute to the needs of the saints (Paul's favorite word for Christians). Practice hospitality. Encourage *one another*. Build up *one another*. It is impossible to do all those things from a *King Me* perspective. When we live with a *King Jesus* perspective we won't forget the outward look.

When we surrender to the **King of the World Culture**, we forget the *upward* look. I picked up a book the other day. I haven't yet had time to read it, but I will soon. The title was what grabbed me—***It's Not About Me***.[115] It reminds me of what has become one of my favorite worship songs in recent years. When I sing Matt Redman's ***The Heart of Worship***[116] I'm reminded why the upward look is essential. If I come to worship with the attitude of that song, then I realize that *my* preferences, *my* passions, *my* place, *my* strengths, *my* weaknesses—anything *mine*—must fade into the background because it is all about Him. There is no room for *King Me* in the heart of a worshiper.

But an hour is coming, and now is, when the true worshipers will worship the Father in spirit and truth; for such people the Father seeks to be His worshipers. God is spirit, and those who worship Him must worship in spirit and truth.[117]

Did you see that? *True worshipers will worship the Father in spirit and truth, for such people the Father seeks to be His worshipers.* That is the key. Worship is not an *activity*, it is an *identity*. *King Me* can attend a worship service. *King Me* cannot be a worshiper. A worshiper of *King Jesus* will not forget the upward look.

When we surrender to the **King of the World Culture**, we distort the *inward* look. *King Me* sees no need for personal transformation. *King Me* perfunctorily attends worship services and Bible studies and even gets involved in ministry projects because he is making brownie points with God and it feels good to be seen doing something good. *King Me* even enjoys the fellowship with others as long as it doesn't interfere with his own agenda. *King Me* may even want to make the world a better place and to see the influence of God affect the culture. But *King Me* doesn't realize that transforming the culture begins with making sure the crown is on the right head.

Therefore, I urge you, brothers, in view of God's mercy, to offer your bodies as living sacrifices, holy and pleasing to God-this is your spiritual act of worship. Do not conform any longer to the pattern of this world, but be transformed by the renewing of your mind. Then you will be able to test and approve what God's will is-his good, pleasing and perfect will.[118]

A spiritual Jedi has as his or her goal transformation of the culture—conquering the evil empire of the Dark Side. But transformation of the culture begins not with changing the world, but with personally rejecting worldly patterns. Personally rejecting worldly patterns begins with personal transformation. Personal transformation begins with a renewed mind focused on pleasing God and doing His will in every area of life. A mind so focused on *King Jesus* will not distort the inward look.

These things I have spoken to you while abiding with you. But the Helper, the Holy Spirit, whom the Father will send in My name, He will teach you all things, and bring to your remembrance all that I said to you. Peace I leave with you; My peace I give to you; not as the world gives do I give to you. Do not let your heart be troubled, nor let it be fearful.[119]

The Jedi's Pledge: I refuse to claim a throne, a crown, and a kingdom that do not belong to me. I reject the **King of the World Culture**. I choose to be a worshiper of King Jesus only and always.

Light Saber Focus: Romans 12:1—*Therefore, I urge you, brothers, in view of God's mercy, to offer your bodies as living sacrifices, holy and pleasing to God-this is your spiritual act of worship.*

Surrender to the Force: Lord Jesus, today I need a renewed mind. I offer myself as a living sacrifice to You for the glory of Your kingdom and Your name. In the name of Jesus I pray, Amen.

Epilogue

Before we wave goodbye with a heartfelt, *Live long and prosper* (oops, wrong movie), I need to make something clear.

This book has not been written by a Jedi Master.

In fact, I'm not sure I even know one. These are the observations of one apprentice writing to others. I have learned the ways of the Jedi from observing others who are more surrendered to the Force than I am yet. I have learned from observing those who appear so natural with the light saber that it seems a part of them. I have learned the hard lessons from my own struggles and stumbles into the Dark Side. But with each renewed surrender, with each new sensation of the light saber in my hand and in my heart, I come away wiser, stronger, and humbled by the grace of the One who is Master and Force and Friend.

The battle is not over, the Jedi are needed. Remember you are not alone. *May the Force be with you.*

Credits

Gerry Lewis wears many hats: pastor…speaker…worship leader…singer/songwriter…author…community leader… neighbor…friend…son…husband…father. Since 1984, he has been married to his best friend, Eva, an elementary school counselor. He is also the exceedingly proud father of Tova, a college freshman, and Zeke, a high school sophomore.

His education includes a Bachelor of Music Education from West Texas A&M University, a Master of Divinity from Southwestern Baptist Theological Seminary and a Doctor of Ministry from Golden Gate Baptist Theological Seminary. In 2007, he will celebrate thirty years in ministry (and his forty-sixth birthday).

Since 1991, he has lived in the same house in the small city of Azle, Texas, serving as Senior Pastor of the Eagle Mountain Baptist Church. Being in the same community for over fifteen years has created many opportunities to interact with the culture of the community. His philosophy of writing is the same as his philosophy of living—*to be a blessing to as many people as possible and demonstrate the character of Jesus Christ in words, actions, and attitudes.* He has served on numerous boards and is a frequent speaker at local churches and other organizations. He has also served five terms as the president of the local interdenominational ministerial alliance. His community involvement was recognized in 2006 when the Azle Area Chamber of Commerce named him Citizen of the Year.

Besides writing, preaching, singing, and songwriting, he enjoys camping, hiking, cooking, photography, and a good cup of coffee.

For information on his writing or subscription to his email devotional, *Life Matters*, go to www.lifematterstoday.com.

For information about his other ministries and resources, go to www.thatllpreach.com.

Mail contact:
Dr. Gerry Lewis
That'll Preach Ministries/Life Matters Publications
P.O. Box 263
Azle, TX 76098

End Notes

Introduction: May the Force Be With You

1   I was actually in the audience at a conference when I heard him use this phrase.
2   John 17:11-21, NASU
3   Proverbs 22:28, NIV
4   Genesis 1:26-28, NASU
5   Genesis 2:7-9, NASU
6   Genesis 2:18-19, NASU
7   John 14:25-28, NASU
8   Ephesians 6:17-18, NLT
9   Hebrews 4:12, NIV

Chapter 1: Road Rage Culture

10   Mick Jagger, quoted in O Timothy, June 2001
11   Evangelical Missions Quarterly, January 2002
12   Barna Research, December 2001
13   Mark 3:1-5, TEV
14   Revelation 14:9-10, NASU
15   Ephesians 4:26-27, NASU
16   Galatians 5:19-21, NLT

17 Ephesians 4:31-32, NLT
18 Colossians 3:8, NLT
19 James 1:19-20, NLT
20 John 14:25-28, NASU

Chapter 2: Wal-Mart Culture

21 Mike Bellah, *Baby Boom Believers: Why We Think We Need It All and How to Survive When We Don't Get It*, Tyndale House, 1988.
22 Mark 10:45, NLT
23 Galatians 6:7-10, NLT
24 2 Corinthians 9:6-12, NLT
25 3/29/04 issue
26 2/7/05 cover story
27 Rick Warren, *The Purpose Driven Life: What on Earth Am I Here For*, Zondervan, 2002.
28 The Prayer of St. Francis
29 Luke 9:23-25, NLT
30 John 14:25-28, NASU

Chapter 3: PG-13 Culture

31 information from www.filmratings.com
32 Genesis 2:24-25, NIV
33 Song of Solomon 7:1-13, NLT
34 James 3:5-8, TEV
35 Paul Robertson, "Helping teens make healthy decisions" youthculture@2000, Fall 2000. Page 13
36 Job 31:1, NIV

37 James 1:26, NASU
38 Ephesians 5:3-4, NASU
39 Ephesians 4:29, NIV
40 Isaiah 50:4, NIV
41 Romans 12:17-21, NASU
42 Philippians 4:8-9, NLT
43 John 14:25-28, NASU

Chapter 4: Divorce Culture

44 Information found at ww.adoptioninstitute.org/research/newnetARC.html
45 Malachi 2:16, NASU
46 Mark 10:2-9, NASU
47 John 3:16-17, NLT
48 Romans 5:8, NIV
49 John 8:10-11, NKJV
50 Ecclesiastes 5:4-6, NASU
51 William Shakespeare, From Romeo and Juliet, II, ii, 1-2
52 Larry L. Bumpass and James A. Sweet. NATIONAL SURVEY OF FAMILIES AND HOUSEHOLDS: WAVE I, 1987-1988, AND WAVE II, 1992-1994 [Computer file]. ICPSR06906-v1. Madison, WI: University of Wisconsin, Center for Demography and Ecology [producer], 1997. Ann Arbor, MI: Inter-university Consortium for Political and Social Research [distributor], 1997.
53 Linda J. Waite, Don Browning, William J. Doherty, Maggie Gallagher, Ye Luo, and Scott M. Stanley, "Does Divorce Make People Happy? Findings from a

Study of Unhappy Marriages," Institute for American Values, July 11, 2002, p. 4. www.americanvalues.org
54 Christine A. Johnson, Scott M. Stanley, Norval D. Glenn, Paul R. Amato, Steve L. Nock, Howard J. Markman, M. Robin Dion, Marriage in Oklahoma, 2001 Baseline Statewide Survey on Marriage and Divorce, a project of the Oklahoma Marriage Initiative, Oklahoma State University Bureau for Social Research, 2001, p. 3. www.okmarriage.com
55 Hebrews 12:1-3, NASU
56 *I Want to Be Happy*, from *No, No Nanette*, Vincent Youmans, composer, Irving Caesar and Otto Harbach, lyricists, 1925
57 John 14:6, NASU
58 Colossians 3:1-4, NASU
59 Albert E. Brumley, *This World is Not My Home*, 1936
60 John 14:25-28, NASU

Chapter 5: Blame Game Culture

61 http://en.wikipedia.org/wiki/Steve_Bartman
62 I made that up, please don't call that number
63 http://www.snopes.com/legal/twinkie.htm
64 Genesis 3:1-13, NASU
65 see Chapter 3—The **PG-13 Culture**
66 Genesis 2:16
67 2 Corinthians 5:10, NIV
68 1 Corinthians 10:13, NIV
69 Colossians 3:23-25, NIV
70 Galatians 6:1-5, NIV
71 John 14:25-28, NASU

Chapter 6: Adrenaline Culture

72 The American Heritage® Dictionary of the English Language, Fourth Edition Copyright © 2004, 2000 by Houghton Mifflin Company. Published by Houghton Mifflin Company.

73 Psalm 4:4, NKJV

74 NASU—Matthew 11:15; Matthew 13:9; Matthew 13:43; Mark 4:9; Mark 4:23; Mark 7:16; Luke 8:8; Luke 14:35; Revelation 2:7: Revelation 2:11; Revelation 2:17; Revelation 2:29; Revelation 3:6; Revelation 3:13; Revelation 3:22; Revelation 13:9

75 1 Kings 19:1-18, NIV

76 Psalm 46:10, NASU

77 Matthew 11:28-30, NIV

78 Isaiah 40:31, TEV

79 John 14:25-28, NASU

Chapter 7: Pffft! Culture

80 Letter To the Editor, Azle News, January 21, 1993

81 Letter To the Editor, Azle News, Feb 4, 1993

82 All these are random names, by the way

83 Judges 21:25, TEV

84 Alan Loy McGinnis, *The Friendship Factor*, Augsburg Publising House, 1979, p. 21

85 Genesis 2:18-25, NLT

86 Leviticus 18:22, NIV

87 Romans 1:26-27, NLT

88 Exodus 20:12, NIV (Also Deuteronomy 5:16; Ephesians 6:2)

89   Leviticus 19:32, NLT
90   1 Timothy 5:3-4, NASU
91   1 Peter 2:17-18, NASU (Also Romans 13:7)
92   1 Peter 2:17, NASU (Also Romans 12:10, 17)
93   Hebrews 13:4, NLT
94   Ephesians 5:33, NLT
95   1 Peter 3:7, NLT
96   1 Samuel 2:30-31, NIV
97   Isaiah 29:13-14, TEV
98   Lamentations 4:16, NASU
99   Malachi 1:6-9, NLT
100 Romans 1:21-22, NASU
101 James 3:8-11, NASU
102 Proverbs 3:35, NIV
103 Proverbs 11:16, NASU
104 Proverbs 15:33, NLT (Also Proverbs18:12; 29:23;
     Luke 14:7-10)
105 Proverbs 21:21, NLT (Also Proverbs 22:4; Romans 2:10)
106 2 Timothy 2:21-22, NASU
107 Ephesians 5:21-6:4, NLT
108 John 14:25-28, NASU

Chapter 8: King of the World Culture

109 Acts 20:32-35, NLT
110 Matthew 7:12, NASU
111 Genesis 3:1-5, NIV
112 John 13:34-35, NASU
113 Romans 12:10-13, NASU

114 1 Thessalonians 5:11, NASU
115 Max Lucado, *It's Not About Me: Rescue from the Life We Thought Would Make Us Happy*, Integrity Publishers, 2004.
116 Matt Redman, *The Heart of Worship*, Thankyou Music, 1997
117 John 4:23-24, NASU
118 Romans 12:1-2, NIV
119 John 14:25-28, NASU

Also available from PublishAmerica

SLEEP TIGHT
by Barbara Wagner

Attractive Caryl Stewart, a western artist, has inherited a fortune and fallen in love with David Eagle, the confident and sensual man of her dreams. When her flamboyant, oil-rich great-aunt, Savannah Buckman, dies, the young redhead travels from Scottsdale, Arizona, to manage her great-aunt's estate in upscale Winter Park near Oklahoma City. After a disturbing secret from Savannah's past is revealed and a manipulative friend, almost Caryl's exact twin, becomes the third victim, Caryl knows she is the target of a cunning killer, an unknown murderer who is slowly going insane. Tormented by Oklahoma wind and trapped in the eerie atmosphere of a mysterious mansion, she struggles to escape from a maze of terror, revenge and murder. When her Native American lover is accused, Caryl makes a startling discovery and a cruel psychopath prepares to combine her death with his pleasure.

Paperback, 289 pages
6" x 9"
ISBN 1-60610-096-3

About the author:

Both a writer and an artist, Barbara Wagner lives with her husband in a suburb of Kansas City close to their grown children. She grew up in Oklahoma, has a degree in fine art from the University of Oklahoma, and studied creative writing at Butler University in Indianapolis. An award-winning artist, her work was marketed in Scottsdale, Arizona, for many years. Though *Sleep Tight* is entirely a work of fiction, the artistic life of the novel's protagonist, Caryl Stewart, is drawn from Barbara's own experience and adds a strong framework to the suspenseful story.

Available to all bookstores nationwide.
www.publishamerica.com

EMILLEE KART AND THE SEVEN SAVING SIGNS

THE TALE OF BEASLEY'S BONNET

by Vanessa Wheeler

From the minute she met her eccentric missionary aunt, Emillee Kart's life would never be the same. During their first lunch at the Butterfly Café, Emillee is inducted into a secret club known as the Monarch's Army; minutes later she is running for her life. Not only is Emillee launched into an age-old battle between the Skywalkers and the Hexiums, she may very well be the key to saving the Earthtreadors. Twelve years ago, on the day Emillee was born, a prophecy spread throughout the land of a child that would turn the tide of the battle. Five children were born on that day; two have disappeared. The Hexiums will stop at nothing to eliminate any threat to their victory. Emillee needs to learn who she is in order to help uncover the clues that will bring the Skywalkers closer to their goal.

Paperback, 202 pages
5.5" x 8.5"
ISBN 1-4241-8597-1

About the author:

Love of fantasy combined with spiritual conviction guided this mother of three to spin this faith- based tale. Joanne Strobel-Cort, born in Bethlehem, Pennsylvania, now lives in Summit, New Jersey, with her husband and three children. She works on Wall Street and is a committed Sunday school teacher who relies on faith to meet the challenges of each day.

CAUGHT MIDSTREAM
by Uta Christensen

In *Caught Midstream*, Janos, a successful executive, reveals the untold experiences of his youth quite unexpectedly to Sparrow—a young woman he is attracted to. She is allowed to relive his epic journey and becomes drawn into an unnerving yet moving tapestry of travails and extraordinary events that take place in prisoner-of-war camps deep within Russia. Taken by force at age sixteen from the protective circle of his family in Germany, Janos is tossed into the cataclysmic, last-gasp efforts of World War II. His journey takes him to a place of darkness, where he lives through a near-death experience and goes through physical and emotional starvation, hard labor, and ostracism; yet it also carries him into unlikely places and relationships where friendship, compassion, healing, mentoring, and love can, amazingly, still flourish. As the story unfolds, Janos's journey accelerates from adolescence into manhood. Almost miraculously, Janos survives while vast numbers of his co-travelers perish.

Paperback, 271 pages
6" x 9"
ISBN 1-4241-0967-1

About the author:

Born in Germany, Uta Christensen spent years in Ireland, New Zealand, and Australia but settled permanently in California. Holding a B.A. in English and German literature, she taught English at a community college and was an administrative analyst at the University of California. Her first book, her father's memoir, was published in Germany.